easy one-pot

easy one-pot

over 100 tasty recipes for busy cooks

RYLAND PETERS & SMALL
LONDON · NEW YORK

Designer Iona Hoyle
Editors Delphine Lawrance, Helen Ridge
Production Ros Holmes
Art Director Leslie Harrington
Publishing Director Alison Starling

Indexer Hilary Bird

First published in the USA in 2009
This paperback edition published in 2017
by Ryland Peters & Small
341 East 116th Street
New York NY 10029

www.rylandpeters.com

10 9 8 7 6 5 4 3 2 1

Text © Nadia Arumugam, Ghillie
Basan, Maxine Clark, Ross Dobson,
Clare Ferguson, Liz Franklin, Tonia
George, Rachael Anne Hill, Louise
Pickford, Jennie Shapter, Sonia
Stevenson, Linda Tubby, Sunil Vijayaker,
Fran Warde, Laura Washburn and
Ryland Peters & Small 2009, 2017

Design and photographs
© Ryland Peters & Small 2009, 2017

ISBN 978-1-84975-828-4

US Library of Congress Cataloging-in-
Publication Data has been applied for.

Printed in China

Notes

• All spoon measurements are level
unless otherwise specified.

• Eggs are large unless otherwise
specified. Uncooked or partly cooked
eggs should not be served to the
very young, the very old, those with
compromised immune systems, or
to pregnant women.

contents

introduction

After a long day at work, the last thing on a lot of people's minds is cooking. It's not merely the thought of having to come up with an idea, but the fact that cooking creates mess. *Easy One-Pot* comes to the rescue of any reluctant cook, providing easy-to-follow recipes, with most of them cooked in just the one pot, pan, or wok, resulting in minimum fuss and little clearing up. What is more, the recipes call for easily sourced as well as relatively inexpensive ingredients.

Easy One-Pot is divided into eight sections. Choose from a variety of Soups, salads, and light bites, including pasta with melted ricotta and harrira. Omelets, tortillas, and frittatas are ready in no time, with tantalizing combinations such as artichoke and ham tortilla or bell pepper and chorizo. For a more oriental flavor, the Noodles and stir-fries section covers delights such as pad thai and five-spice duck with eggplant and plums.

Nothing beats a comforting risotto or rice dish on a cold winter's night. Choose from a plethora of dishes in the Risottos and paellas section, with treats such as artichoke and pecorino risotto or lamb pilaf. Mouthwatering Curries and tagines include an eggplant, tomato, and lentil curry for vegetarians, and a spicy chicken tagine, bringing a taste of Morocco to the dining table.

Creamy dishes like potato gratin are included in the Bakes and gratins section, along with hearty options such as baked stuffed pumpkin. Casseroles and stews are the ultimate warming dish to feed a family. More than 25 recipes are included here, from lemony chicken with leeks to Caribbean vegetable stew and from easy fish stew to Vietnamese-style beef. The joy of one pot extends to desserts, with a fig and honey croissant pudding and a white chocolate and raspberry fool among the options.

Easy One-Pot is the perfect solution for low-fuss yet hearty suppers to be shared among family or friends, and will appeal to meat eaters and vegetarians alike.

soups, salads, & light bites

The trick with tomato soup is to get a bit of acidity fighting back against the natural sweetness of the tomato. For this, you need sweet tomatoes, but to be sure you can add some brown sugar to compensate—it's up to you to decide how much. The vinegar will then cut through this sweetness.

tomato soup

Put the onions, garlic, and oil in a large saucepan, cover, and cook over low heat for 10 minutes, stirring occasionally until soft. Do not let it brown.

Add the tomatoes, sugar, vinegar, and stock and season well. Bring to a boil, then turn down the heat and simmer for 30 minutes, stirring occasionally.

Transfer to a blender in batches and liquidize until really smooth.

Ladle the soup into bowls and drizzle with chili oil, if using.

2 red onions, chopped

3 garlic cloves, crushed

¼ cup extra virgin olive oil

5 lb. plum tomatoes, roughly chopped

1–2 tablespoons soft light brown sugar

2 tablespoons red wine vinegar

3 cups vegetable stock

sea salt and freshly ground black pepper

chili oil, to serve (optional)

serves 4

This soup is sold all over Morocco. At Ramadan, when most of the country is fasting, there is an eerie silence in the usually bustling souks as stall vendors tuck into their harrira, their first meal after sunset. It can be as rustic as you like, but this version is defined by the subtle flavor of saffron and accompanying spices.

harrira

Heat the oil in a heavy-based casserole dish, then add the lamb and brown evenly. Add the onions, celery, garlic, cinnamon, saffron, ginger, and nutmeg, and season well. Turn the heat down a little, cover, and cook for 10 minutes until soft, stirring occasionally.

Stir in the tomato paste and the tomatoes and cook for a further 2–3 minutes. Add the stock, cover, and cook for 1 hour until the lamb starts to become tender.

Add the chickpeas and lentils and cook for a further 40 minutes until they are tender and the lamb can easily be pulled off the bone. Shred the meat from the shank, remove the bone, and discard. Add lemon juice to taste and check the seasoning (it needs quite a generous amount of salt). Stir in the cilantro.

Ladle the soup into bowls and garnish with cilantro leaves.

2 tablespoons extra virgin olive oil

a 1-lb. lamb shank

2 onions, sliced

3 celery ribs, chopped

3 garlic cloves, chopped

1 teaspoon ground cinnamon

½ teaspoon saffron threads

½ teaspoon ground ginger

several gratings of nutmeg

1 tablespoon tomato paste

4 tomatoes, chopped

2¾ cups lamb stock or water

14-oz. can chickpeas, drained and rinsed

½ cup green lentils, rinsed

freshly squeezed juice of 1 lemon

2 tablespoons chopped fresh cilantro

sea salt and freshly ground black pepper

cilantro leaves, to garnish

serves 4–6

This meal-in-a-bowl soup is loosely based on ribollita, the Tuscan vegetable and bread soup. It's one of those recipes that has three essential elements—good oil, fresh vegetables, and good bread. The rest is interchangeable, according to the seasons and your own fancy.

italian vegetable & bread soup

Preheat the oven to 400°F.

Drizzle the ciabatta slices with a little of the oil and bake in the preheated oven for 5–6 minutes, or until crisp. Remove from the oven and set aside.

Meanwhile, heat 3 tablespoons of the oil in a large saucepan and sauté the onions, celery, carrots, and garlic over low heat for 4–5 minutes, or until the vegetables are shiny and starting to soften. Add the tomatoes and cook for a further couple of minutes.

Pour in the stock and cook for 15 minutes. Add the cannellini beans and cook for a further 5 minutes. Add the zucchini, kale, and savoy cabbage and cook for a further 4–5 minutes, or until the greens are just cooked but still retain their color.

Break the ciabatta into bite-size pieces and divide equally between warmed soup bowls. Ladle the soup into the bowls and add a good grinding of pepper. Drizzle with a little more oil and serve immediately.

6 slices of ciabatta bread

about ⅓ cup extra virgin olive oil

2 red onions, chopped

2 celery ribs, chopped

2 carrots, chopped

2 garlic cloves, crushed

6 ripe tomatoes, seeded

6 cups vegetable stock

2 x 14-oz. cans cannellini beans, drained and rinsed

4 zucchini, sliced

6½ oz. kale, chopped

3½ oz. savoy cabbage, shredded

freshly ground black pepper

serves 4

Instead of adding a little fried bacon or pancetta to your minestrone, which is common practice, you can always use Parmesan rind. Buy the cheese in a big chunk and hang on to the rinds in an airtight container in the fridge. Use them for soups like this that need a strong undercurrent; they will add a similar depth of flavor and saltiness.

minestrone soup

¼ cup extra virgin olive oil, plus extra to serve

2 carrots, chopped

1 red onion, chopped

4 celery ribs, diced and leaves reserved

6 garlic cloves, sliced

2 tablespoons freshly chopped flatleaf parsley

2 teaspoons tomato paste

14-oz. can chopped tomatoes

4 cups hot chicken stock or vegetable stock

14-oz. can borlotti beans, drained and rinsed

Parmesan rind (optional)

5 oz. cavolo nero or spring greens, shredded

3½ oz. spaghetti, broken up

sea salt and freshly ground black pepper

freshly grated Parmesan, to serve

serves 4–6

Heat the oil in a large, heavy-based saucepan, then add the carrots, onion, celery, and garlic. Cover and cook very slowly over low heat, stirring occasionally, until thoroughly softened.

Add the parsley, tomato paste, and canned tomatoes and cook for 5 minutes. Pour in the hot stock and borlotti beans and bring to a boil. If using a Parmesan rind, add this now. Once boiling, add the cavolo nero and simmer for 20 minutes.

Add the spaghetti and cook for 2–3 minutes less than the manufacturer's instructions suggest (by the time you have ladled it into bowls it will be perfectly cooked). Taste and add seasoning if it needs it.

Ladle the soup into bowls and drizzle with extra oil. Serve with a bowl of grated Parmesan to sprinkle over the top.

This is Lebanese in origin, but soups like this are served all over the Middle East. Crispy fried onions are a lovely topping, but you have to be brave and really brown them so they look almost black. In order to do this without burning them, you have to really soften them to start with.

lentil, spinach, & cumin soup

Heat the oil in a large, heavy-based saucepan and add the onions. Cook, covered, for 8–10 minutes until softened. Remove half the onion and set aside.

Continue to cook the onion left in the pan for a further 10 minutes until deep brown, sweet, and caramelized. Take out and set aside for the garnish.

Return the softened onion to the pan and add the garlic, coriander, cumin seeds, and lentils and stir for 1–2 minutes until well coated in oil. Add the stock, bring to a boil, then turn down to a gentle simmer for 30 minutes until the lentils are lovely and soft.

Add the spinach and stir until wilted. Transfer half the soup to a blender and liquidize until you have a purée. Stir back into the soup. Season with lemon juice, salt, and pepper.

Ladle the soup into bowls, add a dollop of Greek yogurt, and scatter the pine nuts and fried onions over the top.

3 tablespoons extra virgin olive oil

2 onions, sliced

4 garlic cloves, sliced

1 teaspoon ground coriander

1 teaspoon cumin seeds

¾ cup brown or green lentils

5 cups vegetable stock

6½ cups spinach

freshly squeezed juice of 1 lemon

sea salt and freshly ground black pepper

¼ cup Greek yogurt, to serve

¼ cup pine nuts, lightly toasted, to serve

serves 4

Buy only the freshest and best-quality fish for this classic Mediterranean dish. Ask the fish seller to clean, scale, and fillet the fish, and do make sure that he removes all the scales. Good bouillabaisse also features other seafood such as shrimp, mussels, and clams. If you're feeling rich, you can always add a lobster.

bouillabaisse

½ cup olive oil

1 large onion, diced

2 leeks, thinly sliced

2 garlic cloves, crushed and chopped

1 small head of Florence fennel, diced

3 cups tomato purée

4 cups fish stock

a sprig of thyme

1 fresh bay leaf

a pinch of saffron threads

4 lb. fish and shellfish, cleaned, scaled, and filleted

sea salt and freshly ground black pepper

warm crusty bread, to serve

serves 4

Heat the oil in a large skillet. Add the onion, leeks, garlic, and fennel and sauté the vegetables gently for 5 minutes without letting them brown.

Add the tomato purée, fish stock, thyme, bay leaf, saffron, salt, and pepper. Bring to a boil and simmer for 10 minutes.

Add the pieces of fish and shellfish and cook for 4 minutes.

Carefully lift out the fish fillets and shellfish and divide between 4 large bowls. Ladle over the rich tomato liquid and serve with warm crusty bread.

One of those reliable recipes that just gets better as it matures, ratatouille can be served with many dishes, and also by itself with lots of crusty bread. Don't use green bell peppers—they are too bitter. Traditionally, eggplant was salted to reduce the bitterness, but if you're really pushed for time, don't bother—today, most types rarely need salting.

ratatouille

Cut the eggplant into large, bite-size pieces, put them in a colander, sprinkle well with salt, and let drain for 1 hour. Cut the peppers in half, remove the white membrane and seeds, and slice the flesh into thick strips.

Heat the oil in a heatproof casserole dish and sauté the onions, garlic, and coriander seeds until soft and transparent, but not colored. Add the wine and boil to reduce.

Meanwhile, rinse and drain the eggplant and dry on paper towels. Add the peppers and eggplant to the casserole and cook for about 10 minutes, stirring occasionally until softening around the edges, but not browning. Add the tomatoes, sugar, and olives. Heat to simmering point, season well with salt and pepper, then partially cover with a lid and cook for about 25 minutes. Serve hot or cold. Garnish with basil, if using.

2 eggplant

3 bell peppers (red, yellow, or orange)

3 tablespoons olive oil

2 large onions, thinly sliced

2 garlic cloves, crushed

2 teaspoons finely crushed coriander seeds

⅓ cup white wine

14-oz. can chopped tomatoes

1 teaspoon sugar

about 20 dry-cured kalamata olives

sea salt and freshly ground black pepper

basil leaves, to garnish (optional)

serves 6

Mushroom fans will love this tasty mix of juicy mushrooms in a sweet-and-sour chile-pepper spiked marinade. It makes a perfect side dish for barbecues. Add a crumbling of salty cheese and you have a pretty special vegetarian entrée, too.

marinated mushrooms

¼ cup extra virgin olive oil

2 shallots, finely chopped

2 garlic cloves, crushed

1 lb. cremini mushrooms, halved

1½ tablespoons apple cider vinegar

2 tablespoons raisins

2 tablespoons honey

a pinch of dried chile flakes

fresh oregano leaves, to garnish (optional)

serves 4–6

Heat 3 tablespoons of the oil in a skillet and sauté the shallots and garlic over low heat for 2–3 minutes, until softened. Add the mushrooms and sauté gently for 4–5 minutes, until golden. Add the cider vinegar and raisins, and bubble for a minute or so. Stir in the honey, remaining olive oil, and chile flakes. Cook for a further minute. Remove from the heat and let cool. Marinate for half an hour before serving. Garnish with oregano, if using.

Cornmeal makes a lovely crumb coating on these patties. If using canned tuna, buy a good-quality brand that has a dense texture and large chunks. Alternatively, pan-cook fresh tuna and flake it yourself.

tuna patties

Cook the sweet potatoes in a pan of simmering water for 20 minutes. Drain well and mash. Add the tuna, scallions, and egg, season and mix well. Divide the mixture into 8 equal pieces and shape into patties.

Put the cornmeal on a plate and dip the patties in it until coated on all sides.

Heat the oil and sauté the patties on each side until golden. Serve with lemon wedges and a tomato salad.

20 oz. sweet potatoes, peeled and chopped

10 oz. tuna, flaked

2 scallions, chopped

1 egg

¾ cup cornmeal

3 tablespoons olive oil

sea salt and freshly ground black pepper

1 lemon, cut into wedges, to serve

tomato salad, to serve

serves 4

Pasta is the archetypal fast food. This dish is fast and fresh, with the ricotta melting into the hot pasta and coating it like a creamy sauce. The pine nuts give it crunch, while the herbs lend a fresh, scented flavor. If you don't have all the herbs listed here, use just arugula plus one other—the parsley or basil suggested, or perhaps snippped chives.

pasta with melted ricotta

12 oz. dried penne or other pasta

⅓ cup extra virgin olive oil

1 cup toasted pine nuts, about 4 oz.

4 oz. arugula, chopped

2 tablespoons freshly chopped flatleaf parsley

2 tablespoons freshly chopped basil

8 oz. ricotta cheese, about 1 cup, mashed

4 oz. freshly grated Parmesan cheese

sea salt and freshly ground black pepper

serves 4

Cook the pasta according to the instructions on the package. Drain, reserving ¼ cup of the cooking liquid, and return both to the pan.

Add the toasted pine nuts and their oil, the herbs, ricotta, half the Parmesan, plenty of black pepper, and salt to taste. Stir until the pasta is evenly coated.

Serve in warmed bowls, with the remaining cheese sprinkled on top.

For those nights when you want dinner in a hurry, this savory dish can be on the table in just 10 minutes. Serve with basmati and wild rice or couscous, together with some green beans or cabbage.

mustardy mushroom stroganoff

Cook the onion in a covered saucepan with 3 tablespoons of the stock for about 4 minutes or until softened and the liquid has evaporated.

Stir in the mushrooms, garlic, and seasoning, then add the remaining stock, mustard, and tomato paste. Cook, covered, for 2 minutes, then remove the lid and cook rapidly for 2 minutes to reduce the liquid to a syrup.

Remove from the heat. Stir in the sour cream and parsley. Serve immediately on a bed of rice or couscous with green beans or cabbage.

½ small onion, sliced

⅔ cup vegetable stock

5 oz. mixed mushrooms, chopped if large

1 garlic clove, crushed

1 teaspoon whole-grain mustard

½ teaspoon tomato paste

1 tablespoon sour cream

sea salt and freshly ground black pepper

freshly chopped flatleaf parsley, to serve

serves 1

There's no dressing as such for this dish because the roasting chorizo produces a wonderful paprika-scented oil. The juices should be really hot so they wilt the spinach slightly. With the sweet potato, meaty chorizo, and salty cheese, this is much more than a salad.

sweet potato salad

1¼ lb. sweet potatoes, peeled and cut into wedges

2 tablespoons extra virgin olive oil

2 fresh rosemary sprigs, broken up into smaller sprigs

½ teaspoon dried red pepper flakes

8 oz. chorizo, sliced

3 tablespoons sherry vinegar

6½ oz. fresh baby spinach

½ cup black olives, pitted and chopped

6 oz. feta cheese, cut into large chunks

serves 4

Preheat the oven to 375°F.

Place the sweet potatoes in a roasting pan, drizzle with the oil, and sprinkle with the rosemary and red pepper flakes. Roast for 10 minutes until beginning to soften.

Add the chorizo and roast for a further 15 minutes until the chorizo is crisp and the sweet potato is softening and blackening nicely.

At the end of the cooking time, drizzle over the vinegar and return to the oven for a further 5 minutes.

Put the spinach in bowls and top with the sweet potato, chorizo, olives, and feta. Drizzle the juices from the roasting pan over the salad and stir well before serving.

Many Thai salads, soups, and stews are flooded with the pungent flavors of Thai basil, mint, and cilantro. Thai basil is readily available from most Asian stores, but you could use regular basil instead.

thai-style beef salad

Put the peppercorns, coriander, and salt onto a plate and mix. Rub the beef all over with the oil and then put onto the plate and turn to coat with the spices.

Cook the beef in a stovetop grill pan or skillet for about 10 minutes, turning to brown evenly. Remove from the heat and let cool.

Meanwhile, to make the dressing, put the sugar into a saucepan, add the fish sauce and 2 tablespoons water, and heat until the sugar dissolves. Let cool, then stir in the lime juice, chiles, and garlic.

Cut the beef into thin slices and put into a large bowl. Add the cucumber, scallions, bok choy, and herbs. Pour over the dressing, toss well, then serve.

1 tablespoon black peppercorns, lightly crushed

1 teaspoon ground coriander

1 teaspoon sea salt

1 lb. whole beef fillet

1 tablespoon peanut or canola oil

1 cucumber, thinly sliced

4 scallions, thinly sliced

2 baby bok choy, thinly sliced

a handful of freshly chopped Thai basil

a handful of freshly chopped mint

a handful of freshly chopped cilantro

lime dressing

1 tablespoon palm sugar or brown sugar

1 tablespoon Thai fish sauce

2 tablespoons lime juice

2 small, hot red chile peppers, seeded and chopped

1 garlic clove, crushed

serves 4

This is a wonderfully colorful dish, with yellow from the saffron, red from the tomato, and green from the basil. The potatoes absorb the glorious golden color and subtle flavor of the saffron as they simmer gently with the tomatoes. Serve warm, as the heat will release the heady aromas of the basil and saffron.

saffron potato salad

1 lb. large waxy yellow-fleshed potatoes, peeled

a pinch of saffron threads, about 20

8 sun-dried tomatoes (the dry kind, not in oil)

caper & basil dressing

6 tablespoons extra virgin olive oil

3 tablespoons freshly chopped basil leaves, plus extra to serve

2 tablespoons salted capers, rinsed and chopped, if large

1–2 tablespoons freshly squeezed lemon juice, to taste

sea salt and freshly ground black pepper

serves 4

Cut the potatoes into large chunks. Put in a saucepan, add enough cold water to just cover them, then add the saffron and sun-dried tomatoes. Bring slowly to a boil, then turn down the heat, cover, and simmer very gently for about 12 minutes until just tender. If the water boils too fast, the potatoes will start to disintegrate. Drain well.

Pick out the now plumped-up sun-dried tomatoes and slice them thinly. Tip the potatoes into a large bowl and add the sliced tomatoes.

To make the dressing, put the oil, chopped basil, and capers in a small bowl. Add lemon juice, salt, and pepper to taste and mix well. Pour over the hot potatoes, mix gently, then serve hot or warm, scattered with extra basil leaves.

In Italy, this dish is traditionally made with white cannellini beans, but green flageolet beans make an attractive alternative. Fresh tuna can be expensive, so this is a good way of making one wonderful steak stretch a little further.

italian tuna & beans

If using fresh tuna, brush with olive oil and put in a preheated stovetop grill pan. Cook for 3 minutes on each side or until barred with brown but pink in the middle (the cooking time will depend on the thickness of the fish). Remove from the pan, cool, and cut into chunks.

Put the oil, onions, garlic, and vinegar in a bowl and beat with a fork. Add the beans and toss until well coated.

Add the tuna and basil, salt, and pepper. Serve with crusty bread.

1 large tuna steak, about 9 oz., or 2 small cans good-quality tuna, about 6 oz. each, drained

6 tablespoons olive oil, plus extra for brushing

2 red onions, finely sliced

2–3 large garlic cloves, crushed

1 tablespoon sherry vinegar or white wine vinegar

3 x 14-oz cans green flageolet beans or white cannellini beans, drained and rinsed, or a mixture of both

4 handfuls of fresh basil leaves and small sprigs

sea salt and freshly ground black pepper

crusty bread, to serve

serves 4–6

Strictly speaking, this isn't a recipe for the traditional Chinese dish but a variation, using a prepared rotisserie chicken, but you could substitute smoked chicken breasts or even roast duck from a favorite Chinese restaurant.

bang-bang chicken

a 5¼ lb. prepared rotisserie chicken

3 carrots, peeled and shredded

1 small cabbage, shredded

3 mixed bell peppers, cut into strips

1 cup sugar snap peas, diagonally halved

3 tablespoons toasted sesame oil

⅓ cup sesame seeds

sauce

1 cup peanut butter

3–4 tablespoons chili sauce

1 inch fresh ginger, peeled and grated

3 tablespoons toasted sesame oil

2 tablespoons extra virgin olive oil

serves 4

Put the chicken on a chopping board. Using a rolling pin, give the chicken a few good thwacks along the breast. This will make it much easier to shred. Shred the meat into a large bowl.

Mix together the carrots, cabbage, bell peppers, and sugar snap peas in four individual bowls. Top with the shredded chicken.

Heat the sesame oil in a small skillet and sauté the sesame seeds until golden.

To make the sauce, put the peanut butter, chili sauce, ginger, sesame oil, and olive oil in a saucepan, beat to combine, and heat gently over low heat.

Drizzle some of the sauce over the chicken and scatter with the sesame seeds. Serve immediately, with the remaining sauce alongside.

The creamy horseradish dressing in this recipe is a fabulous complement to the richness of the smoked mackerel, while raw vegetables add crunch and color. If you wish, you can use couscous instead of bulgur wheat.

mackerel & bulgur wheat salad

Cook the bulgur wheat in a saucepan of lightly salted boiling water for 15 minutes or until tender. Drain, then mix with the lemon juice, chives, yellow pepper, and radishes.

Put the spinach leaves into shallow salad bowls, spoon the bulgur wheat on top, then add the flaked smoked mackerel. Mix the dressing ingredients together and drizzle over the fish. Finish with a grinding of black pepper to serve.

½ cup bulgur wheat

1 tablespoon freshly squeezed lemon juice

1 tablespoon finely snipped fresh chives

½ yellow bell pepper, seeded and diced

8 radishes, sliced

1½ cups fresh baby spinach

5 oz. smoked mackerel fillets, flaked

dressing

3 tablespoons sour cream

2 teaspoons horseradish sauce

1 teaspoon finely snipped fresh chives

freshly ground black pepper, to serve

serves 2

Dried fenugreek leaves, known as methi in Indian food stores, are not as easy to find as the seeds, but they have a unique flavor that scents the dish and makes it something out of the ordinary. If you can't find methi, use dried mint instead, or omit altogether. Use enough chiles to suit your taste.

spicy chickpeas

1 tablespoon peanut or mustard oil

2 teaspoons ground turmeric

2 teaspoons black mustard seeds

2 onions, chopped

2 garlic cloves, chopped

1 tablespoon dried fenugreek leaves (optional)

4 tomatoes, peeled, halved and seeded

3–5 fresh red chiles, halved, seeded if preferred, then chopped

2 x 14 oz. cans chickpeas, drained and rinsed

sea salt, to taste

fresh fenugreek leaves, to serve (optional) *

serves 4

Heat the oil in a casserole dish, add the turmeric and mustard seeds, and heat until the seeds pop. Add the onions and garlic and sauté gently until softened and lightly browned. Add the dried fenugreek leaves, if using, tomatoes, and chiles. Cook at a low heat until the tomatoes have melted down to form a sauce.

Add the chickpeas to the casserole dish. Turn to coat with the mixture and cook until hot. Add salt to taste. Serve, topped with sprigs of fresh fenugreek leaves, if using.

* Fresh fenugreek leaves are sold in Indian greengrocers. They are cooked and served like spinach, but a few sprigs make a delicious garnish. Omit if they are hard to find.

omelets, tortillas, & frittatas

A whole breakfast made without fuss in one pan. Use the best bacon you can find and fresh, free-range eggs. It's made like a giant omelet—almost an Italian frittata.

bacon & eggs in a pan

Set a large, nonstick skillet over medium heat. Add the oil, heat, then add the bacon. Cook for 2 minutes until the bacon starts to brown and go crisp around the edges.

Break the eggs into a bowl, add salt and pepper, and whisk lightly. Pour into the skillet around the bacon, making sure the base is covered and the bacon sits half-submerged. Dot with the tomatoes and cook over medium to low heat until the eggs have set. Sprinkle with chives and serve immediately, cut into wedges.

1 tablespoon safflower oil

8 slices bacon

6 extra-large eggs

10 cherry tomatoes, halved

2 tablespoons snipped fresh chives

sea salt and freshly ground black pepper

serves 4

This omelet is fast to make, nice to look at, and easy to eat. Add some sliced sausages if you like, and serve hot or cold, with mixed salad greens and crusty bread or pita.

greek-style omelet

1 cup cherry tomatoes, halved

4–5 pickled golden hot peppers, drained and sliced

3 scallions, sliced

⅓ cup pitted black olives, sliced

4 oz. feta cheese

a small handful of freshly chopped flatleaf parsley

6 extra-large eggs

sea salt and freshly ground black pepper

olive oil, for the pan

salad

8 oz. mixed salad greens

1 tablespoon freshly squeezed lemon juice (a little less than ½ lemon)

¼ cup extra virgin olive oil

sea salt and freshly ground black pepper

serves 2–4

Preheat the oven to 400°F.

Rub a deep skillet with olive oil, then arrange the tomatoes, pickled peppers, scallions, and olives equally around it. Crumble in the feta, then grind pepper over the top. Sprinkle with parsley.

Put the eggs in a bowl, beat well, and season with a good pinch of salt. Pour over the ingredients in the pan. Bake in the preheated oven until puffed and just golden around the edges, 15–20 minutes.

To make the salad, put the leaves in a bowl, add the lemon juice, oil, salt, and pepper. Toss well, taste, and adjust the seasoning with more salt and pepper if necessary. Serve with the omelet cut into wedges—hot, warm, or at room temperature.

Traditionally, a Spanish tortilla is made with potatoes and onions, but this quicker variation uses bell peppers and chorizo. You could, though, use just onions, any kind of cheese, tomatoes, zucchini, ham, or salami. Experiment! This is good for breakfast, brunch, lunch, dinner, or a late-night snack, and can be served hot or cold.

bell pepper & chorizo tortilla

Heat the oil in a large, nonstick skillet. Add the bell peppers and onion and cook over medium-high heat until golden brown, 3–5 minutes. Add the garlic and chorizo, cook for 2–3 minutes. Season with a pinch of salt and set aside.

Beat the eggs in a bowl. Stir in the parsley, season with ¼ teaspoon salt, and pepper to taste, then pour over the bell peppers in the pan. Sprinkle with the cheese.

Cover and cook over low heat until set around the edges but still barely wobbly in the middle, 10–12 minutes. Loosen the sides and underneath with a plastic spatula. You should be able to slide the tortilla out of the pan and onto a plate, then flip onto another plate to serve bottom-side up. If it cannot be shaken out of the pan, put a large plate upside down over the skillet, hold the edges with oven mitts, and flip over to release the tortilla. Serve hot, warm, or cold.

2 tablespoons extra virgin olive oil

1 red bell pepper, thinly sliced

1 yellow bell pepper, thinly sliced

1 onion, thinly sliced

2 garlic cloves, chopped

4 oz. chorizo or pepperoni, sliced

6 extra-large eggs

a handful of freshly chopped flatleaf parsley

½ cup freshly grated Manchego cheese

sea salt and freshly ground black pepper

serves 4–6

The traditional tortilla must be one of the world's most accommodating dishes. It's good for almost any occasion—picnic food, a quick lunch dish eaten between slices of bread, even a breakfast snack—and this variation, which includes garlic, is no exception. Served with a scarlet sweet pepper sauce, it is delicious.

spanish potato omelet

2 tablespoons extra virgin olive oil

2 lb. boiling potatoes, peeled and cut into 1-inch cubes

1 onion, sliced into rings

4 garlic cloves, finely chopped (optional)

6 eggs, beaten

¼ cup freshly chopped flatleaf parsley or scallion tops

sea salt and freshly ground black pepper

piquillo sauce

8-oz. jar or can of roasted sweet peppers, such as piquillos or pimientos

3 tablespoons sherry vinegar

serves 4–6

Heat the oil in a medium skillet, add the potatoes and onion, and cook over low heat for 12–14 minutes or until tender but not browned, moving them about with a spatula so that they cook evenly. Add the garlic, if using, for the last 2 minutes.

Put the eggs in a bowl, beat well, and season with salt and pepper.

Using a slotted spoon, remove the cooked potatoes, onion, and garlic from the skillet and stir them into the egg mixture. Stir in the parsley.

Quickly pour the mixture back into the hot skillet. Cook, not stirring, over low to moderate heat for 4–5 minutes or until firm, but do not let it brown too much. The top will still be wobbly, only part-cooked.

Holding a plate over the top of the omelet, quickly invert the skillet, omelet, and plate. Slide the hot omelet back, upside down, to brown the other side for 2–3 minutes more, then remove from the skillet and let cool for 5 minutes.

To make the sauce, put the sweet peppers, ⅓ cup of the liquid from the jar (make it up with water if necessary) and the sherry vinegar in a blender. Purée to form a smooth, scarlet sauce.

Cut the omelet into chunks, segments, or cubes. Serve the sauce separately, spooning some over the pieces of tortilla.

Ideal for a lunch or supper dish, or perfect for al fresco dining served with a crisp salad, this omelet is just bursting with flavor. It is worth buying tomatoes ripened on the vine for their extra taste explosion.

feta cheese & tomato open omelet

Break the eggs into a bowl and beat lightly with a fork, just enough to mix the yolks and whites. Season with salt and pepper, add 2 tablespoons water, and the basil, mint, and scallions and mix briefly.

Heat the oil in an omelet pan. Pour in the egg mixture and cook over medium heat for 4–5 minutes, drawing the mixture from the sides to the center until the omelet is half cooked.

Top with the feta and the tomato halves, cut side up, and cook for 2 minutes. Slide under a preheated broiler and cook until light golden brown. Slide onto a warmed plate and serve immediately.

5 extra-large eggs

2 tablespoons freshly chopped basil

1 tablespoon freshly chopped mint

3 scallions, finely chopped

2 tablespoons safflower oil

¾ cup (3 oz.) crumbled feta cheese

8 small cherry tomatoes, halved

sea salt and freshly ground black pepper

serves 2

This frittata has a real Mediterranean feel and is flavored with some of Italy's favorite ingredients—olives, sun-dried tomatoes, and Parmesan. If you have the time, it is worth mixing the tomatoes and sage into the eggs up to an hour before cooking for a more intense flavor.

sun-dried tomato frittata

6 extra-large eggs

8 sun-dried tomatoes in oil, drained and sliced

1 tablespoon freshly chopped sage

⅓ cup thickly sliced pitted black olives

½ cup (2 oz.) freshly grated Parmesan cheese, plus extra shavings to serve (optional)

2 tablespoons extra virgin olive oil

1 onion, halved and sliced

sea salt and freshly ground black pepper

serves 2–3

Break the eggs into a large bowl and beat lightly with a fork. Add the sun-dried tomatoes, sage, olives, Parmesan, some salt and pepper and mix gently.

Heat the oil in a large nonstick skillet, add the onion, and cook over low heat until soft and golden.

Increase the heat to moderate, pour the egg mixture into the skillet, and stir just long enough to mix in the onion. Cook over medium-low heat until the base of the frittata is golden and the top has almost set.

Slide the skillet under a preheated broiler to finish cooking, or put a plate on top of the skillet, then invert so the frittata drops onto the plate. Return the frittata to the skillet, cooked side up, and cook on top of the stove for 1–2 minutes.

Transfer to a serving plate, top with Parmesan shavings, if using, and serve hot or cold, cut into wedges.

Porcini are difficult to buy fresh, but are widely available dried. They are one of the best mushrooms, with an intense, rich flavor that will pervade the omelet. Strain the soaking liquid from the porcini and add a spoonful to the omelet mixture, or keep it for a soup or stew.

porcini frittata

Put the porcini in a small bowl and cover with warm water. Let soak for 30 minutes. Break 1 of the eggs into a bowl, add the mascarpone, and mix well. Add the remaining eggs and beat lightly with a fork. Stir in the parsley and season with salt and pepper.

Heat 1 tablespoon of the oil in a large nonstick skillet, add the onion, and cook over low heat until soft. Add another tablespoon of oil and the white mushrooms and cook for 5 minutes. Drain the porcini and chop if large. Add to the pan and cook for 2 minutes.

Using a slotted spoon, transfer the mushrooms and onions into the egg mixture and stir gently.

Wipe out the skillet with a paper towel, add the remaining oil, and heat gently. Add the frittata mixture and cook over low heat until browned on the underside and nearly set on top. Sprinkle with Parmesan and slide under a preheated broiler to finish cooking the top and melt the cheese. Transfer to a warm serving plate.

Melt the butter in the skillet, add the wild mushrooms, and sauté quickly. Spoon over the top of the frittata and serve.

½ oz. dried porcini mushrooms

6 large eggs

3 tablespoons mascarpone cheese

3 tablespoons freshly chopped flatleaf parsley

3 tablespoons extra virgin olive or safflower oil

1 onion, halved and sliced

2½ cups (4 oz.) sliced small white mushrooms

1 tablespoon freshly grated Parmesan cheese

1 tablespoon unsalted butter

3 oz. fresh wild mushrooms

sea salt and freshly ground black pepper

serves 2–3

A specialty of the Alicante region of Valencia is an unusual meat paella finished with an omelet topping. For this mouthwatering tortilla, the meat has been replaced with shellfish typical of Paella Valenciana.

paella tortilla

3 tablespoons extra virgin olive or safflower oil

1 skinless chicken breast, about 6 oz., cut into strips

1 medium onion, chopped

1 garlic clove, chopped

1 red bell pepper, halved, seeded, and sliced

2 tomatoes, chopped

½ cup calasparra (paella) rice

a pinch of saffron threads, soaked in 2 tablespoons hot water

1 cup chicken stock

1½ cups (6 oz.) ready-mixed seafood, such as shrimp, mussels, and squid rings *

6 large eggs

3 tablespoons frozen peas, thawed

sea salt and freshly ground black pepper

serves 4–6

Heat 2 tablespoons of the oil in a large nonstick skillet, add the chicken, and sauté until browned. Transfer to a plate.

Add the onion, garlic, and bell pepper and sauté for 5–6 minutes, stirring frequently, until softened.

Stir in the tomatoes, rice, and saffron and pour in the stock. Season with salt and plenty of black pepper. Cover and cook over gentle heat for about 20 minutes, or until the rice is almost tender, adding a little more stock if necessary.

Stir in the mixed seafood and chicken and cook for 5 minutes, or until the rice is just tender and all the liquid has been absorbed.

Break the eggs into a large bowl, add salt and pepper, and beat lightly with a fork. Stir the paella mixture and the peas into the eggs.

Wipe out the skillet with a paper towel. Heat the remaining oil in the skillet over medium heat, add the tortilla mixture, and cook over medium-low heat for 10–15 minutes, or until almost set.

Slide under a preheated broiler to set the top. Let stand for 5 minutes, then transfer to a serving plate and serve, cut into wedges.

* If ready-mixed seafood cocktail is unavailable, use ½ cup each of shelled shrimp, shelled mussels, and squid rings.

Chickpeas are a delicious alternative to potatoes in a tortilla, adding a slightly sweet, nutty flavor. This tortilla is quite filling, so is best as a main meal, served with a green salad.

chickpea tortilla

Break the eggs into a large bowl, add the paprika, salt, and pepper, and beat lightly with a fork. Stir in the parsley.

Heat 2 tablespoons of the oil in a large nonstick skillet. Add the onion and bell pepper and cook for about 5 minutes until softened, turning frequently. Add the garlic and chickpeas and cook for 2 minutes.

Transfer the chickpea mixture to the bowl of eggs and stir gently. Add the remaining oil to the skillet and return to the heat. Add the tortilla mixture, spreading it evenly. Cook over medium-low heat until the bottom is golden brown and the top almost set.

Put a plate on top of the skillet and hold it in place. Invert the skillet so the tortilla drops onto the plate. Slide back into the skillet, brown side up, and cook for another 2–3 minutes until lightly browned on the other side. Serve hot or at room temperature, cut into wedges.

5 extra-large eggs

½ teaspoon sweet paprika

3 tablespoons freshly chopped flatleaf parsley

3 tablespoons extra virgin olive oil

1 large onion, finely chopped

1 red bell pepper, halved, seeded, and chopped

2 garlic cloves, finely chopped

2 cups canned chickpeas, drained and rinsed

sea salt and freshly ground black pepper

serves 2–3

Most tortillas are inverted onto a plate and returned to the pan to finish cooking. However, this tortilla is topped with cured mountain ham and should be finished under the broiler. You can trickle a little extra virgin olive oil over the top before broiling and even add a few slices of goat cheese log, which melts beautifully into the top of the tortilla.

artichoke & ham tortilla

3 tablespoons extra virgin olive or safflower oil

3 medium potatoes, about 12 oz., peeled and cubed

1 large onion, chopped

5 extra-large eggs

2 cups (15 oz.) canned artichoke hearts or bottoms in water, well drained and cut in half

2 tablespoons fresh thyme leaves

3–4 oz. thinly sliced serrano ham or prosciutto, torn into strips

6–8 slices goat cheese log with rind, about 4 oz. (optional)

sea salt and freshly ground black pepper

serves 3–4

Heat 2 tablespoons of the oil in a large nonstick skillet. Add the potatoes and sauté over medium heat for 5 minutes. Add the onion and cook for a further 10 minutes, lifting and turning occasionally, until just tender. The potatoes and onions should not brown very much.

Meanwhile, break the eggs into a large bowl, season with salt and pepper, and beat lightly with a fork. Add the artichokes, thyme, and about three-quarters of the ham. Add the potatoes and onion and stir gently.

Heat the remaining oil in the skillet. Add the tortilla mixture, spreading it evenly. Cook over medium-low heat for about 6 minutes, then top with the remaining ham. Cook for a further 4–5 minutes or until the bottom is golden brown and the top almost set.

Add the goat cheese, if using, and slide under a preheated broiler to brown the top, about 2–3 minutes. Serve hot or warm, cut into wedges.

noodles & stir-fries

Pork tenderloin is given a spicy boost with classic Thai flavorings, and the toasted coconut finishes off this super-tasty stir-fry perfectly. If you can't get hold of Thai basil, simply replace with cilantro.

thai-flavor pork

Heat a wok or large skillet until hot. Add the coconut and dry-fry over high heat for a few minutes until golden. Remove from the wok and set aside.

Place the pork tenderloin between 2 large sheets of plastic wrap, then hit with a rolling pin until you have flattened it to about 1 inch. Slice very thinly. Season the pork with salt and pepper.

Heat the oil in the wok, then sear the pork in 2 or 3 batches over high heat, adding more oil if necessary. Remove the pork from the wok and set aside.

Add the ginger, garlic, chiles, and lemon grass to the wok and stir-fry for 1 minute. Return the pork to the wok and stir-fry for 1 minute. Add the chili sauce and fish sauce, and stir well. Cook for a further 2 minutes, or until the pork is completely cooked through. Stir through the Thai basil. Remove from the heat and serve immediately with rice or noodles, garnished with the toasted coconut.

4–5 tablespoons grated fresh coconut (or desiccated, if necessary)

1 lb. 4 oz. pork tenderloin

2 tablespoons vegetable oil

1 teaspoon finely grated fresh ginger

3 cloves garlic, thinly sliced

4 whole fresh bird's-eye chiles

1 stalk lemon grass, outer skin removed and bottom 2 inches bruised

2 tablespoons chili sauce

1 tablespoon fish sauce

a large handful of Thai basil

sea salt and freshly ground black pepper

serves 4

Classic Chinese crispy duck is given an updated twist with an aromatic dry rub of five-spice powder, fresh plums, and meaty eggplant to soak up the tangy sauce. Serve with either noodles or rice.

five-spice duck

2 skinless duck breasts, thinly sliced

1 teaspoon Chinese five-spice powder

2 tablespoons vegetable or peanut oil

1 medium onion, sliced

1 small eggplant, quartered and sliced

2 plums, pitted and cut into wedges

sea salt and freshly ground black pepper

sauce

3 tablespoons Chinese plum sauce

1 tablespoon rice wine vinegar

2 tablespoons clear honey

1 tablespoon dark soy sauce

serves 2–3

Combine all the ingredients for the sauce in a bowl and set aside.

Put the duck in a bowl and sprinkle over the five-spice powder, a sprinkling of salt, and freshly ground pepper. Rub into the duck.

Heat the oil in a wok or large skillet. Add the duck in batches and stir-fry over high heat until sealed all over. Remove the duck from the wok and set aside.

Add the onion to the wok, with a little more oil if necessary, and stir-fry for 2 minutes until softened and golden. Add the eggplant with a good sprinkling of water and stir-fry for 2–3 minutes. Return the duck to the wok and stir well. Add the sauce ingredients, reduce the heat, and simmer for a further 3–4 minutes, covered, until the eggplant is just tender.

Remove the lid, then stir in the plum wedges. Cook for 2 minutes, then check the seasoning, adding more salt or soy sauce if necessary. Serve immediately with noodles or rice.

Why order out when you can knock out this fresh-tasting, healthy take on the perennial Chinese favorite quickly and easily? Don't worry if you can't find Chinese rice wine; use dry sherry instead. Serve with either noodles or rice.

chinese lemon chicken

Combine all the marinade ingredients in a bowl, stir in the chicken, cover, and marinate in the fridge for 20–30 minutes.

Meanwhile, to make the sauce, put all the ingredients in a bowl with 2 tablespoons cold water, stir to combine, and set aside.

Heat a wok or large skillet until hot, then add the sesame seeds and dry-fry over medium heat for about 2 minutes, or until lightly toasted. Remove from the wok and set aside.

Heat 1½ tablespoons of the oil in the wok until very hot. Add the chicken in 2 batches and stir-fry over high heat for 3–4 minutes until golden brown and well sealed all over. Remove the chicken from the wok and set aside.

Add the remaining oil to the wok and add the onion. Stir-fry for 2–3 minutes until softened and golden. Pour in the sauce and bring to a boil, then reduce the heat and simmer for 1 minute.

Return the chicken to the wok and stir through the sauce. Simmer for 2 minutes, or until the chicken is cooked through. Remove from the heat. Serve immediately over noodles or rice. Sprinkle over the toasted sesame seeds and garnish with the scallions.

4 skinless chicken breasts, cut into thin strips

1 tablespoon sesame seeds

2 tablespoons peanut or vegetable oil

1 onion, thinly sliced

2 scallions, green parts only, thinly sliced on the diagonal, to garnish

marinade

1 tablespoon light soy sauce

1 tablespoon Chinese rice wine or dry sherry

2 teaspoons finely grated fresh ginger

2 garlic cloves, crushed

1 teaspoon cornstarch

sauce

⅓ cup chicken stock

freshly squeezed juice and finely grated zest from 1 large unwaxed lemon

3 tablespoons clear honey

1 tablespoon light soy sauce

1 teaspoon toasted sesame oil

2 teaspoons cornstarch

serves 4

Transform everyday vegetables into a memorable meal with a few carefully chosen whole and ground spices. As in many Indian-influenced dishes, a spiky ginger and garlic paste forms the basis of this stir-fry. Why not make extra and store in the fridge or freezer for another day? Serve with either basmati or white long grain rice.

spiced mixed vegetables

1 teaspoon finely grated fresh ginger

2 cloves garlic, crushed

1 tablespoon vegetable oil

½ teaspoon fennel seeds

1 teaspoon cumin seeds

1 onion, halved and sliced

¼ teaspoon ground cumin

¼ teaspoon ground coriander

½ teaspoon ground red chile

⅔ cup canned chopped tomatoes

6½ oz. cauliflower, cut into small florets

2 carrots, cut into 1½ -inch matchsticks

1 cup trimmed green beans, cut on the diagonal into 1½-inch lengths

2 tablespoons chopped cilantro leaves

sea salt

serves 2

Place the ginger and garlic in a blender and whiz to a paste with a little water. Alternatively, grind to a rough paste with a pestle and mortar.

Heat the oil in a wok or large skillet, then add the fennel and cumin seeds and stir-fry over high heat until they start to pop. Add the onion and cook for a further 3–4 minutes, or until golden. Stir in the ginger and garlic paste and continue to cook for a further 2 minutes, stirring. Spoon in the ground cumin, ground coriander, and red chile, and, after a few seconds, the canned tomatoes. Cook over high heat for 1 minute, or until most of the liquid has evaporated.

Add the cauliflower and carrots to the wok with a good sprinkle of water, stir, then cover immediately and cook for 2 minutes.

Add the green beans, season with salt, and cook for a further 2–3 minutes uncovered, until the vegetables are cooked but still a little crunchy. Taste and add more salt if necessary.

Remove from the heat and stir in the chopped cilantro. Serve immediately with rice.

Ideal for quick and casual entertaining, this stir-fry has the deliciously different savory taste of yellow bean sauce and the colorful combination of red and yellow bell peppers. Rice or noodles, tossed with a little toasted sesame oil, is the ideal accompaniment to this dish.

chicken & yellow bean stir-fry

Combine all the marinade ingredients in a bowl, then add the chicken pieces and mix well. Cover and marinate in the refrigerator for 10–15 minutes so that the flavors combine.

When ready to cook, heat the oil in a wok or large skillet until hot, then add the chicken and stir-fry over high heat for 3–4 minutes until golden, well sealed, and nearly cooked through. Remove from the wok and set aside.

Add the bell peppers to the wok and stir-fry briskly over high heat for 2 minutes. Return the chicken to the wok and add the yellow bean sauce. Cook for 1 minute, stirring occasionally.

Meanwhile, combine the soy sauce, chicken stock, and cornstarch in a bowl with 2 tablespoons cold water. Stir until smooth, then pour into the wok. Simmer gently until the sauce has thickened and the chicken is cooked through. Remove from the heat and sprinkle with the almonds, if using. Serve immediately with rice or noodles tossed with a little toasted sesame oil.

2 large skinless chicken breasts, cut into 1-inch pieces

1 tablespoon peanut oil

1 red and 1 yellow bell pepper, seeded and thinly sliced

2 tablespoons yellow bean sauce

½ tablespoon light soy sauce

⅓ cup chicken stock

2 teaspoons cornstarch

1 tablespoon slivered almonds, lightly toasted in a skillet, to garnish (optional)

marinade

½ tablespoon Chinese rice wine or dry sherry

1 tablespoon light soy sauce

1 teaspoon toasted sesame oil

½ teaspoon sugar

1 teaspoon finely grated fresh ginger

a pinch of dried red pepper flakes

serves 2

The fat and chewy wheat-based Japanese udon noodles make this dish wonderfully satisfying. The richly flavored sauce gets its complex undertones from a good dose of oyster sauce, and the tofu and meaty shitake mushrooms absorb it completely for a thoroughly flavorful dish.

tofu & mushroom noodles

14 oz. udon noodles

1 tablespoon vegetable oil

10 oz. firm tofu, cut into
1-inch cubes

1 teaspoon finely grated
fresh ginger

3 scallions, white and light green parts cut into 1-inch lengths and shredded; green parts sliced on the diagonal

1 red chile, seeded and shredded

7 oz. shitake mushrooms, stalks discarded and caps sliced,

sauce

2 tablespoons oyster sauce

1 tablespoon light soy sauce

⅔ cup vegetable stock

1 tablespoon cornstarch combined with 2 tablespoons cold water

serves 2

Bring a saucepan of water to a boil. Add the udon noodles and cook according to the package instructions. Drain and rinse under cold running water. Set aside.

Combine all the sauce ingredients in a bowl and set aside.

Heat the oil in a wok or large skillet. When hot, add the tofu. Cook, stirring gently, until golden all over. Remove the tofu from the wok, and drain on paper towels.

Add the ginger, shredded scallions, and chile to the wok and stir-fry for 1 minute over high heat. Add the mushrooms and cook for 1 more minute, then pour in the sauce and bring to a boil. Reduce the heat, return the tofu to the wok, and simmer gently for 1–2 minutes, or until the sauce has thickened.

Stir the cooked and drained noodles into the sauce very carefully and heat through. Remove from the heat, garnish with the remaining scallions, and serve immediately.

Thai food always presents the palate with a kaleidoscope of flavors and the knack is getting the balance just right. Pad thai needs to be really sweet and soothing, but the tamarind and lime give it a fruity tang of sourness and the fish sauce provides a characteristic salty depth.

pad thai

Soak the noodles according to the instructions on the package, then drain and shake dry. Set aside. Combine the tamarind paste, fish sauce, and sugar then set aside.

Heat the oil in a wok or large skillet over medium heat and add the garlic. Stir-fry until the garlic begins to color, then add the shrimp, peanuts, and red pepper flakes. Stir-fry for another 2–3 minutes, or until the shrimp turn pink and the nuts are golden.

Add the noodles to the wok along with the tamarind mixture. Toss until everything is evenly coated and push to one side of the wok. Pour the egg into a corner of the wok and cook until it is scrambled and dry, then stir into the noodle mixture. Add the beansprouts and scallions, give it one final toss, and transfer to bowls. Serve with a few lime wedges on the side.

6½ oz. flat medium rice noodles

2 tablespoons tamarind paste

3 tablespoons Thai fish sauce

3 tablespoons palm sugar or natural cane sugar

2 tablespoons safflower oil

3 garlic cloves, crushed

8 oz. uncooked tiger shrimp, shelled and deveined but tails intact

⅓ cup unsalted peanuts, chopped

½ teaspoon dried red pepper flakes

2 eggs, beaten

1 cup beansprouts

4 scallions, shredded

lime wedges, to serve

serves 2

Most noodle dishes take just a matter of minutes to cook—in fact, noodles made of rice flour or mung bean starch are ready almost instantly. Wheat-based noodles take the most time—but even then, only about the same as regular pasta.

gingered chicken noodles

2 tablespoons rice wine

2 teaspoons cornstarch

12 oz. skinless chicken breasts

7 oz. Chinese dried egg noodles

3 tablespoons peanut or safflower oil

1-inch fresh ginger, peeled and thinly sliced

4 oz. snow peas, thinly sliced

¼ cup freshly chopped garlic chives or chives

4 oz. cashew nuts, about 1 cup, toasted in a dry skillet, then chopped

sauce

½ cup chicken stock

2 tablespoons dark soy sauce

1 tablespoon freshly squeezed lemon juice

1 tablespoon toasted sesame oil

2 teaspoons light brown sugar

serves 4

Put the rice wine and cornstarch into a bowl and mix well. Cut the chicken into small chunks, add to the bowl, stir well, and set aside to marinate while you prepare the remaining ingredients.

Prepare the noodles according to the instructions on the package, then drain and shake dry.

Put all the sauce ingredients into a small bowl and mix well.

Heat half the oil in a wok or large skillet, then add the chicken and stir-fry for 2 minutes until golden. Remove to a plate and wipe the wok clean with paper towels. Add the remaining oil, then the ginger and snow peas, and stir-fry for 1 minute. Return the chicken to the wok, then add the noodles and sauce. Heat through for 2 minutes.

Add the garlic chives and cashew nuts, stir well, and serve.

To lift your stir-fries out of the ordinary and into the sublime, you need to be a bit crafty with ingredients. Both lemon grass and kaffir lime leaves can be difficult to find, but they freeze well, so keep a few in the freezer for meals such as this. Serve with either steamed rice or egg noodles.

stir-fried asparagus & tofu

Heat the oil in a wok or large skillet over medium/low heat and add the cashew nuts, chiles, lemon grass, lime leaves, garlic, and ginger. Gently sauté for 1 minute.

Add the tofu, asparagus, and bell peppers and stir-fry for a further 2 minutes until they start to soften around the edges and the cashew nuts turn golden.

Add the tamarind paste, soy sauce, and honey, along with ⅓ cup water and turn up the heat to bring the liquid to a boil. Allow the contents of the wok to bubble up so that the liquid finishes cooking the vegetables. This should take a further 3 minutes or so.

Transfer to bowls. Remove the slices of ginger, unless you like hits of feisty ginger! Serve piping hot with steamed rice or egg noodles.

1 tablespoon safflower oil

⅓ cup cashew nuts

2 large red chiles, sliced (and seeded if you prefer it mild)

1 lemon grass stalk (outer layer discarded), finely minced

2 kaffir lime leaves, shredded

2 garlic cloves, crushed

1 inch fresh ginger, sliced

8 oz. silken tofu, cubed

8 oz. medium asparagus tips

2 red bell peppers, cut into strips

1 tablespoon tamarind paste

2 tablespoons dark soy sauce

1 tablespoon clear honey

serves 4

risottos & paellas

Smoky grilled artichokes are wonderful combined with nutty pecorino. Pecorino is made from ewes' milk, and when aged can be grated like Parmesan. When young, it has a Cheddar-like texture and a rich, nutty flavor.

artichoke & pecorino risotto

Cut the artichokes into quarters and set aside.

Melt half the butter in a large, heavy saucepan and add the onion. Cook gently for 10 minutes until soft, golden, and translucent but not browned. Add the rice and stir until well coated with the butter and heated through. Pour in the wine and boil hard until it has reduced and almost disappeared. This will remove the taste of raw alcohol.

Begin adding the stock, a large ladle at a time, stirring gently until each ladle has almost been absorbed by the rice. The risotto should be kept at a bare simmer throughout cooking, so don't let the rice dry out—add more stock as necessary. Continue until the rice is tender and creamy, but the grains still firm. (This should take 15–20 minutes depending on the type of rice used—check the package instructions.)

Taste and season well with salt and pepper, then beat in the remaining butter and all the pecorino. Fold in the artichokes. Cover and let rest for a couple of minutes, then serve immediately. You may like to add a little more hot stock to the risotto just before you serve to loosen it, but don't let it wait around too long or the rice will turn mushy.

12 marinated artichokes

1 stick unsalted butter

1 onion, finely chopped

2⅓ cups risotto rice

⅔ cup dry white wine

about 6 cups hot vegetable stock or chicken stock

¾ cup freshly grated pecorino cheese

sea salt and freshly ground black pepper

serves 4–6

A wonderfully light and fragrant risotto, perfect for the summer to serve with cold chicken or fish. Try to use the more fragrant soft herbs here—the more, the merrier.

green herb risotto

1 stick unsalted butter

8 scallions, green and white parts, finely chopped

⅔ cup dry white wine

finely grated zest and freshly squeezed juice of 1 large unwaxed lemon

2⅓ cups risotto rice

about 6 cups hot vegetable stock or chicken stock

¼ cup freshly chopped herbs such as parsley, basil, marjoram, and thyme

¾ cup freshly grated Parmesan cheese

sea salt and freshly ground black pepper

serves 4–6

Melt half the butter in a large, heavy saucepan and add the scallions. Cook gently for 3–5 minutes until soft. Pour in the wine, add half the lemon zest, and boil hard until the wine has reduced and almost disappeared. This will remove the taste of raw alcohol. Add the rice and stir until well coated with butter and scallions and heated through.

Begin to add the hot stock, a large ladle at a time, stirring until each ladle has been absorbed by the rice. Continue until the rice is tender and creamy, but the grains still firm. (This should take 15–20 minutes depending on the type of rice used—check the package instructions.)

Taste and season well with salt and lots of freshly ground black pepper. Stir in the remaining butter, the lemon zest, juice, herbs, and Parmesan. Cover and let rest for a couple of minutes, then serve immediately. You may like to add a little more hot stock to the risotto just before you serve to loosen it, but don't let it wait around too long or the rice will turn mushy.

A pretty, delicate risotto made even more special with sliced zucchini flowers (squash blossom). The female flowers will produce a zucchini if fertilized, while the male flowers are the ones used for stuffing—the central spike must be removed before cooking. Squash blossoms are sold in Italian produce stores and some farmers' markets.

squash blossom risotto

Melt half the butter in a large, heavy saucepan and add the onion and celery. Cook gently for 10 minutes until soft, golden, and translucent but not browned. Add the rice and stir until well coated with the butter and heated through.

Begin adding the stock, a large ladle at a time, stirring gently until each ladle has almost been absorbed by the rice. The risotto should be kept at a bare simmer throughout cooking, so don't let the rice dry out—add more stock as necessary. Halfway through cooking, stir in the zucchini. Continue cooking and adding stock until the rice is tender and creamy, but the grains still firm. (This should take 15–20 minutes, depending on the type of rice used—check the package instructions.)

Taste, season well with salt and pepper, beat in the remaining butter and all the Parmesan, then stir in the squash blossoms. Cover and let rest for a couple of minutes, then serve immediately. You may like to add a little more hot stock to the risotto just before you serve to loosen it, but don't let it wait around too long or the rice will turn mushy.

1 stick unsalted butter

1 onion, finely chopped

1 celery rib, finely chopped

2 cups risotto rice

about 6 cups hot vegetable stock or chicken stock

4 zucchini, grated

½ cup freshly grated Parmesan cheese

4–6 squash blossoms, trimmed and thinly sliced

sea salt and freshly ground black pepper

serves 4

Any kind of fresh wild mushroom will make this risotto taste wonderful, but it will also work very well with a mixture of cultivated mushrooms and reconstituted dried porcini.

wild mushroom risotto

1 stick unsalted butter

1 large onion, finely chopped

2 garlic cloves, finely chopped

3 cups mixed wild mushrooms, cleaned and coarsely chopped

1 tablespoon chopped fresh thyme

1 tablespoon chopped fresh marjoram

⅔ cup dry white wine or vermouth

2⅓ cups risotto rice

6 cups hot vegetable stock or chicken stock

¾ cup freshly grated Parmesan cheese, plus extra to serve

sea salt and freshly ground black pepper

serves 4–6

Melt the butter in a large, heavy saucepan and add the onion and garlic. Cook gently for 10 minutes until soft, golden, and translucent but not browned. Stir in the mushrooms and herbs, then cook over medium heat for 3 minutes to heat through. Pour in the wine and boil hard until it has reduced and almost disappeared. This will remove the taste of raw alcohol. Stir in the rice and sauté with the onion and mushrooms until dry and slightly opaque.

Begin adding the hot stock, a large ladle at a time, stirring until each ladle has been absorbed by the rice. Continue until the rice is tender and creamy, but the grains still firm. (This should take 15–20 minutes depending on the type of rice used—check the package instructions.)

Taste and season well with salt and pepper. Stir in the Parmesan, cover, and let rest for a couple of minutes. Serve immediately with extra grated Parmesan. You may like to add a little more hot stock to the risotto just before you serve to loosen it, but don't let it wait around too long or the rice will turn mushy.

Salad greens, herbs, and bulgur wheat are combined here with chickpeas in a variation of this Middle Eastern dish. When buying greens, keep in mind you will need about two large handfuls per person. If they wilt a little on the way home, give them a quick bath in a bowl of cold water with a pinch or two of sugar thrown in, to freshen them up.

tabbouleh with chickpeas

Put the bulgur wheat in a heatproof bowl and pour over ½ cup boiling water. Stir once, cover tightly with plastic wrap, and set aside for 8–10 minutes. Put the lemon juice and oil in a small bowl and whisk. Pour over the bulgur and stir well with a fork, fluffing up the bulgur and separating the grains.

Put the bulgur in a large bowl with the parsley, mint, dill, tomatoes, chickpeas, and salad greens. Use your hands to toss everything together. Season well with salt and pepper. Transfer to a serving plate and serve with toasted flatbread, if you like.

½ cup bulgur wheat

2 tablespoons freshly squeezed lemon juice

¼ cup extra virgin olive oil

1 small bunch of flatleaf parsley, finely chopped

1 large handful of mint leaves, finely chopped

2 tablespoons finely snipped dill

1 small basket of cherry tomatoes, halved

14-oz. can chickpeas, drained and rinsed

4–5 oz. spring salad mix

sea salt and freshly ground black pepper

toasted flat bread, to serve (optional)

serves 4

This spicy shrimp dish couldn't be any quicker or simpler to make, and it can even be prepared in advance. On the day, all you need do is make the couscous.

shrimp with couscous

1/4 cup extra virgin olive oil

2 teaspoons ground cumin

1 teaspoon ground ginger

1 teaspoon paprika

1/2 teaspoon cayenne pepper

2 lb. medium uncooked shrimp, shell off

2 garlic cloves, crushed

2 lemons, 1 juiced, 1 cut into wedges for serving

a bunch of cilantro, leaves finely chopped

sea salt and freshly ground black pepper

couscous

1 1/4 cups couscous, about 8 oz.

1/2 teaspoon sea salt

3–4 tablespoons extra virgin olive oil

freshly squeezed juice of 1/2 lemon

serves 4

To prepare the couscous, pour it into a large bowl, add the salt, and mix. Add 1¾ cups boiling water and 1 tablespoon oil. Cover and set aside for about 5 minutes to absorb the water.

Using your fingers, break up the lumps of couscous to air them. Fluff up with a fork and set aside while you make the shrimp.

Heat the oil in a skillet. Add the cumin, ginger, paprika, and cayenne and cook, stirring, for 30 seconds. Add the shrimp, garlic, and a good pinch of salt. Cook, stirring, for 1 minute. Add the juice of 1 lemon and 1 cup water. Stir, then cover and simmer until the shrimp are opaque and cooked through, 3–5 minutes. Remove from the heat and stir in the cilantro. Taste and adjust the seasoning with salt, pepper, and extra lemon juice if necessary.

Transfer the couscous to a serving plate and season with the juice of 1/2 lemon and 2–3 tablespoons oil. Stir well. Put the shrimp on top, sprinkle with their cooking juices, and serve with the lemon wedges.

This dish of jasmine rice and canned crabmeat, with the addition of a few fresh ingredients, is a truly luxurious feast. If you are really looking to impress, then use freshly picked white crabmeat but go easy on the flavorings, as you don't want to overwhelm the delicate sweetness of the crab.

jasmine rice with crab & asparagus

Heat the oil in a wok or large skillet until hot. Add the onion and stir-fry over high heat for 2–3 minutes, or until softened and golden. Add the garlic and chile and cook for a further minute. Add the asparagus stalks and stir-fry for 2 minutes, then add the tips and 2 teaspoons of the soy sauce and stir-fry for 30 seconds. Stir in the crabmeat and heat through.

Mix in the rice, then pour in the chili sauce, sesame oil, and remaining soy sauce. Stir well until everything is thoroughly combined and the rice is piping hot. Taste and check for seasoning, then stir in the chives and remove from the heat. Serve immediately.

1 tablespoon peanut oil

1 small onion, finely chopped

2 garlic cloves, crushed

1 large red chile, seeded and finely chopped

4½ oz. fine asparagus, cut into 1-inch lengths, stalks and tips kept separately

1 tablespoon light soy sauce, plus extra if needed

6½ oz. canned or fresh white crabmeat, well drained

1½ cups cold, cooked jasmine rice

1 tablespoon sweet chili sauce

¼ teaspoon toasted sesame oil

2 tablespoons snipped chives

serves 2

Paella is made in countless variations in different areas of Spain, depending on local ingredients and styles. Traditional combinations include rabbit with snails, and pork ribs with cauliflower and beans, and an all-vegetable paella is also popular these days. Don't stir paella constantly like risotto.

chicken & pork paella

8 chicken drumsticks and thighs, mixed, or 1 whole chicken, about 3 lb., cut into pieces

2 teaspoons sea salt

freshly ground black pepper

4 teaspoons paprika

¼ cup extra virgin olive oil

3–4 boneless pork chops, or 12 oz. salt pork cut into 1-inch cubes

2 onions, chopped

4 garlic cloves, crushed

1 lb. tomatoes, fresh or canned, peeled, seeded, and chopped

2 large pinches of saffron threads

1¾ cups calasparra (paella) rice

3–3½ cups hot chicken stock or vegetable stock

1 cup frozen peas, thawed

6 oz. green beans, halved

8 baby artichokes, halved lengthwise, or canned or marinated equivalent

8 large uncooked shrimp, shell on

serves 4–6

Pat the chicken dry with paper towels. Put 1 teaspoon each of salt, pepper, and paprika in a bowl and mix well. Sprinkle the chicken with half the mixture and toss well.

Heat the oil in a large, shallow skillet. Add the chicken and pork, in batches if necessary, and sauté over medium heat for 10–12 minutes or until well browned. Remove with a slotted spoon and set aside.

Add the onions, garlic, tomatoes, and saffron to the pan, then add the remaining salt and paprika. Cook until thickened, about 5 minutes. Stir the mixture well, then replace the meats, stir in the rice and most of the hot stock. Cook over high heat until bubbling fiercely, then reduce the heat and simmer gently, uncovered, for 15 minutes.

Add the peas, beans, artichokes, shrimp, and remaining stock, if necessary, and continue to cook for 10–15 minutes more or until the rice is cooked and glossy but dry. Serve the paella straight from the skillet.

This technique of cooking rice is Middle Eastern in origin but it has spread far and wide—similar rice dishes can be found in European, Asian, Latin American, Caribbean, and Indian cuisines, and it is known by many names, including pilau, pilav, and pulao.

orange vegetable pilaf

Put the oil in a heavy-based saucepan set over high heat. Add the onion, garlic, ginger, and chile and cook for 5 minutes, stirring often. Add the spices and almonds and cook for a further 5 minutes, until the spices become aromatic and look very dark in the pan.

Add the rice and cook for a minute, stirring well to coat the rice in the spices. Add the carrot, pumpkin, and sweet potato to the pan. Pour in 2½ cups water and stir well, loosening any grains of rice that are stuck to the bottom of the pan. Bring to a boil, then reduce the heat to low, cover the pan with a tight-fitting lid, and cook for 25 minutes, stirring occasionally.

Add the lime juice and cilantro, stir well to combine, and serve.

2 tablespoons olive oil

1 onion, chopped

2 garlic cloves, chopped

1 tablespoon finely grated fresh ginger

1 large red chile, finely chopped

1 teaspoon ground coriander

1 teaspoon ground cumin

1 teaspoon turmeric

½ cup slivered almonds

1½ cups basmati rice

1 carrot, cut into large chunks

7 oz. pumpkin or squash, peeled, seeded, and cut into wedges

1 small sweet potato, peeled and cut into thick half-circles

freshly squeezed juice of 1 lime

1 handful of fresh cilantro leaves

serves 4

This vegetarian take on a classic Spanish paella is colorful, delicious, and bursting with fresh, young summer vegetables grown on the vine and enhanced with the subtle flavor of saffron. Perfect for summer entertaining.

vegetarian paella

a large pinch of saffron threads

⅓ cup olive oil

7 oz. red or yellow cherry tomatoes

4 oz. green beans

4 baby zucchini, halved

3 oz. frozen peas, thawed

2 garlic cloves, chopped

2 fresh rosemary sprigs

1½ cups calasparra (paella) rice

3⅓ cups vegetable stock

¼ cup slivered almonds, lightly toasted

serves 4

Put the saffron in a bowl with ⅓ cup hot water and set aside to infuse. Heat half of the oil in a heavy-based skillet set over high heat and add the tomatoes. Cook for 2 minutes, shaking the skillet so that the tomatoes soften and start to split. Remove the tomatoes from the skillet with a slotted spoon and set aside. Add the beans, zucchini, and peas and stir-fry over high heat for 2–3 minutes. Set aside with the tomatoes.

Add the remaining oil to the skillet with the garlic and rosemary, and cook gently for 1 minute to flavor the oil. Add the hot stock and saffron water to the skillet, then stir in the rice. Cook over high heat until bubbling fiercely, then reduce the heat and simmer gently, uncovered, for about 20 minutes until almost all the stock has been absorbed.

Scatter the cooked tomatoes, beans, zucchini, and peas over the rice, cover lightly with some foil, and cook over low heat for 5 minutes so that the vegetables are just heated through. Sprinkle the almonds on top to serve.

This vegetarian dish comes from Valencia, where it is served during the Lenten fast. Its Spanish name—arroz al horno con perdiz—means "rice with partridge," although the partridge is really a whole bulb of garlic.

baked rice with garlic

Preheat the oven to 350°F.

Heat the oil in a heatproof shallow casserole dish or skillet with an ovenproof handle. Add the garlic bulb and onion and sauté for 12 minutes over low heat until the garlic is pale golden and beginning to soften and the onion soft and golden.

Remove the garlic and reserve. Increase the heat and add the tomatoes and juices. Cook until the mixture starts to thicken a little. Stir in the paprika, and salt and pepper to taste.

Stir in the rice. Add half the stock or water and bring slowly to a boil. Add the chickpeas, drain the raisins, and gently fold them into the rice. Put the garlic in the center and bake in the preheated oven for 10 minutes. Heat the remaining stock or water, then add as much as the rice seems to need. Continue baking for 10–15 minutes before serving, covering the top with foil if it seems to be over-browning or drying out. Serve from the casserole dish.

1½ cups olive oil

1 garlic bulb, left whole, skin on

1 large onion, finely chopped

4 tomatoes, peeled, seeded, and chopped (keep the juices)

1 teaspoon sweet paprika

2 cups calasparra (paella) rice

up to 1 quart vegetable stock or water

2 cups canned chickpeas, drained and rinsed

⅓ cup raisins, soaked in hot water for 30 minutes until plump

sea salt and freshly ground black pepper

serves 6

This makes a great mid-week supper dish. Feel free to increase your vegetable intake by adding vegetables of your choice. Frozen peas, corn kernels, or green beans are particularly useful, as they cook in minutes and don't require any preparation.

shrimp & lima bean rice

1 tablespoon olive oil

1 cup basmati rice

1 large onion, chopped

1 teaspoon ground turmeric

14 oz. canned chopped tomatoes

1 large red bell pepper, seeded and finely chopped

1–2 garlic cloves, chopped

2 cups chicken stock

14 oz. canned lima beans, drained and rinsed

1–2 red chiles, seeded and thinly sliced

1 lb. cooked peeled shrimp, thawed if frozen

3 tablespoons fresh cilantro, coarsely chopped

sea salt and freshly ground black pepper

serves 4

Heat the oil in a large nonstick saucepan. Add the rice, onion, and turmeric and cook over medium heat, stirring, for 2 minutes. Add the tomatoes, bell pepper, garlic, stock, and salt and pepper, to taste. Cover the pan with a tight-fitting lid, reduce the heat, and simmer for 15 minutes, until most of the stock has been absorbed by the rice.

Add the lima beans, chiles, and shrimp to the rice mixture and stir through gently. Replace the lid and cook for a further 3 minutes, or until the stock is absorbed and the shrimp are thoroughly warmed through. Stir in the cilantro and serve immediately.

Variation Brown four skinned, boneless chicken thighs in the oil, then add to the rice and onion and proceed as above. Add some frozen peas and corn kernels with the lima beans and shrimp and cook for 3–5 minutes, or until cooked and piping hot. Serve with lemon wedges, if you like.

This protein-packed salad is ideal for lunch. It uses brown basmati rice, which releases its sugars into the bloodstream at a very slow rate throughout the afternoon.

saffron fish pilaf

Heat the oil in a large skillet, add the onion and garlic, if using, and sauté gently for 3 minutes. Add the rice and continue to sauté, stirring, for 2 minutes. Add the saffron powder and stir well. Pour in half the stock, bring to a boil, then reduce the heat and simmer gently for about 25 minutes, stirring occasionally, adding more stock as it is absorbed by the rice.

Add the fish, peas, corn, and tomatoes, stir well, and cook for a further 5–10 minutes. Add the cilantro and pepper, to taste, then cook for 5 minutes more until the rice is tender.

Top with the hard-cooked egg, then serve.

Variation Replace the fish with 10 oz. chopped ham and ½ cup chopped fresh pineapple.

2 teaspoons olive oil

1 onion, chopped

2–3 garlic cloves, crushed (optional)

¾ cup brown basmati rice, rinsed

¼ teaspoon saffron powder

3–4 cups vegetable stock

12 oz. white fish, such as cod fillet, skinned if necessary and cut into small pieces

3½ oz. undyed smoked haddock fillet, skinned and cut into small pieces (optional)

⅓ cup frozen peas

⅓ cup frozen corn kernels

1 lb. tomatoes, chopped

1 tablespoon chopped fresh cilantro

2 hard-cooked eggs, shelled and quartered

freshly ground black pepper

serves 4–6

This pilaf is typical of many Middle Eastern dishes that combine dried fruit and nuts as well as grains and meat. The golden raisins and dried apricots give an underlying sweetness to the dish.

lamb pilaf

3 tablespoons olive oil

1 onion, chopped

2 garlic cloves, crushed

5 cardamom pods, crushed

1 cinnamon stick

3 bay leaves

⅓ cup blanched almonds

1 lb. lamb stewing meat, cut into 1-inch pieces

⅓ cup golden raisins

⅓ cup dried apricots

2 cups basmati rice

a handful of chopped fresh parsley (optional)

serves 4

Heat 1 tablespoon of the oil in a large skillet, add the onion and garlic, and fry for 5 minutes. Add the cardamom, cinnamon, bay leaves, and almonds, and cook for a further 4 minutes. Transfer to a plate.

Heat the remaining oil and fry the lamb on high heat until browned all over. Return the onion mixture to the pan along with the raisins and dried apricots. Pour in just enough water to cover, then bring to a boil, cover, and simmer for 1½ hours.

Add the rice, stir well, and cover with water. Bring to a boil, then cover and simmer very gently for 30 minutes. Add the parsley, if liked, and serve.

curries & tagines

A tagine is a Moroccan stew as well as the earthenware pot in which the dish is traditionally cooked. The stew is usually made with either meat or poultry, gently simmered with vegetables, olives, preserved lemons, garlic, and spices.

chicken & olive tagine

In a bowl, mix together all the ingredients for the marinade. Put the chicken thighs or legs in a shallow dish and coat them in the marinade, rubbing it into the skin. Cover and chill in the refrigerator for 1–2 hours.

Heat the olive oil with the butter in a tagine or heavy-based casserole dish. Remove the chicken pieces from the marinade and brown them in the oil. Pour over the marinade that is left in the dish and add enough water to come halfway up the sides of the chicken pieces. Bring to a boil, reduce the heat, cover with a lid, and simmer for about 45 minutes, turning the chicken from time to time.

Add the preserved lemon, olives, and half the thyme to the tagine. Cover again and simmer for a further 15–20 minutes. Check the seasoning and sprinkle the rest of the thyme over the top. Serve immediately from the tagine.

8–10 chicken thighs
or 4 whole legs

1 tablespoon olive oil with
a pat of unsalted butter

2 preserved lemons, cut into strips

6 oz. cracked green olives

1–2 teaspoons dried thyme
or oregano

sea salt and freshly ground
black pepper

marinade

1 onion, grated

3 garlic cloves, crushed

a 1-inch piece of fresh ginger,
peeled and grated

a small bunch of cilantro, finely
chopped

a pinch of saffron threads

freshly squeezed juice of 1 lemon

1 teaspoon sea salt

3–4 tablespoons olive oil

serves 4

The rosemary and ginger of this spicy and fruity tagine give it a delightful aroma. It can be made with chicken pieces, pheasant, or duck, and needs only a buttery couscous and salad greens to accompany it.

spicy chicken tagine

2 tablespoons olive oil with a pat of unsalted butter

1 onion, finely chopped

3 sprigs of rosemary, 1 finely chopped, the other 2 cut in half

a 1½-inch piece of fresh ginger, peeled and finely chopped

2 red chiles, seeded and finely chopped

1–2 cinnamon sticks

8 chicken thighs

¾ cup dried apricots

2 tablespoons clear honey

14-oz. can plum tomatoes with their juice

sea salt and freshly ground black pepper

a small bunch of fresh green or purple basil leaves, the larger leaves shredded

serves 4

Heat the oil and butter in a tagine or heavy-based casserole dish. Stir in the onion, chopped rosemary, ginger, and chiles and sauté until the onion begins to soften.

Stir in the halved rosemary sprigs and the cinnamon sticks. Add the chicken thighs and brown them on both sides. Toss in the apricots with the honey, then stir in the tomatoes with their juice. (Add a little water, if necessary, to ensure there is enough liquid to cover the base of the tagine and submerge the apricots.) Bring the liquid to a boil, then reduce the heat. Cover with a lid and cook gently for 35–40 minutes.

Season to taste with salt and pepper. Sprinkle the basil over the chicken and serve the dish immediately with couscous and salad greens.

Summer tagines using seasonal vegetables are often quite light and colorful. Other vegetables that might be added to this recipe include tomatoes, eggplant, and peas. This dish is particularly good served with wedges of lemon to squeeze over it and a fresh green salad of baby beet greens, spinach, and lettuce leaves.

summer tagine of lamb

Heat the oil in a tagine or heavy-based casserole dish. Stir in the onion, garlic, cumin and coriander seeds, dried mint, and ginger. Once the onions begin to soften, toss in the meat and pour in enough water to just cover it. Bring the water to a boil, reduce the heat, cover with a lid, and cook gently for about 1½ hours.

Season the cooking juices with salt and pepper. Add the zucchini, bell pepper, and tomatoes, tucking them around the meat (add a little more water if necessary). Cover with a lid again and cook for about 15 minutes, until the zucchini and bell pepper are cooked but retain a bite.

Toss in some of the parsley and fresh mint, sprinkle the rest on top, and serve immediately with lemon wedges and a green salad.

3–4 tablespoons olive oil

1 onion, roughly chopped

4 garlic cloves, roughly chopped

1 teaspoon cumin seeds

1 teaspoon coriander seeds

1 teaspoon dried mint

a 1-inch piece of fresh ginger, peeled and finely chopped

1½ lb. lean lamb, cut into bite-size pieces

2 small zucchini, sliced thickly on the diagonal

1 red or green bell pepper, seeded and cut into thick strips

4 tomatoes, peeled, seeded, and cut into chunks

a small bunch of fresh flatleaf parsley, roughly chopped

a small bunch of fresh mint leaves, roughly chopped

sea salt and freshly ground black pepper

1 lemon, cut into quarters, to serve

serves 4–6

Shoulder of lamb suits this sweet, spicy tagine perfectly, because it is one of the sweeter cuts of meat. Like all stews made with aromatic spices, it tastes even better the next day, once the flavors have mingled. Serve with couscous.

lamb & fava bean tagine

2½ lb. boneless shoulder of lamb or shoulder chops, cut into large chunks

2 teaspoons ground cinnamon

2 teaspoons ground cumin

½ teaspoon hot ground red pepper

1 teaspoon ground turmeric

a pinch of saffron threads

½ teaspoon ground white pepper

2 tablespoons olive oil

3 onions, chopped

3 garlic cloves, crushed

2½ cups hot lamb stock

1 cup dates, pitted

1 cup fava beans, shelled

sea salt

cilantro, to garnish

serves 4

Put the lamb in a large bowl and toss with the cinnamon, cumin, ground red pepper, turmeric, saffron, and white pepper. Heat 1 tablespoon oil in a tagine or heavy-based casserole dish over high heat, then add half the lamb. Cook for a few minutes, stirring occasionally, until the lamb is evenly brown. Tip into a bowl, add the rest of the oil to the tagine dish, and brown the remainder of the lamb. Put all the lamb back in with the onions, garlic, stock, and a large pinch of salt. Bring the mixture to a boil, cover with a lid, and reduce the heat. Simmer gently for 1 hour.

Add the dates to the tagine and simmer for a further 20 minutes.

Add the fava beans and simmer for a further 10 minutes. The tagine should have been cooking for 1½ hours and the meat should be so tender that it falls apart easily. Garnish with cilantro and serve with buttered couscous.

This vegetarian tagine is best made with baby eggplant, but you can also use slender, larger eggplant cut into quarters lengthwise. As a main dish, it is delicious served with couscous or bulgur wheat, and a dollop of thick, creamy yogurt. It can also be served as a side dish to accompany meat or poultry.

tagine of baby eggplant

Heat the oil and butter in a tagine or heavy-based casserole dish. Stir in the onions and garlic and sauté until they begin to color. Add the chiles, coriander and cumin seeds, and sugar. When the seeds give off a nutty aroma, toss in the whole baby eggplants, coating them in the onion and spices. Tip in the tomatoes, cover with a lid, and cook gently for about 40 minutes, until the eggplants are beautifully tender.

Season to taste with salt and pepper and add half the mint and cilantro leaves. Cover and simmer for a further 5–10 minutes. Sprinkle with the remaining mint and cilantro and serve hot with couscous or bulgur wheat and a dollop of yogurt.

1–2 tablespoons olive oil

1 tablespoon unsalted butter

1–2 red onions, halved lengthwise and sliced with the grain

3–4 garlic cloves, crushed

1–2 red chiles, seeded and sliced, or 2–3 dried red chiles, left whole

1–2 teaspoons coriander seeds, roasted and crushed

1–2 teaspoons cumin seeds, roasted and crushed

2 teaspoons sugar

16 baby eggplants, with stalks intact

2 x 14-oz. cans chopped tomatoes

a bunch of fresh mint leaves, roughly chopped

a bunch of cilantro, roughly chopped

sea salt and freshly ground black pepper

serves 4

The authentic flavor of a curry comes from using fresh spices (not ones that have been lurking in your very own kitchen graveyard) and the heady, slightly sour taste of bay leaves. Chicken thighs work better here than breast meat, as they are harder to overcook. Warm chapattis and mango chutney make good accompaniments.

chicken & lentil curry

2 tablespoons unsalted butter

2 large onions, thinly sliced

2 garlic cloves, crushed

1½ tablespoons garam masala

1 lb. boneless chicken thigh or breast meat, cut into chunks

1¼ cups tomato purée

8 bay or curry leaves

⅔ cup red lentils

1¾ cups chicken stock

sea salt and freshly ground black pepper

cilantro leaves, to garnish (optional)

cucumber yogurt

⅔ cup plain yogurt

¼ cucumber, cut into ribbons or chopped

serves 4

Melt the butter in a deep skillet, add the onions, and sauté, stirring, over medium heat. Once they are sizzling, cover with a lid, reduce the heat, and cook for 10–15 minutes, stirring occasionally.

When the onions have softened, add the garlic and garam masala, cook for a further 3–4 minutes until the spices start to release their aroma and the onions are beginning to turn golden. If you are using chicken thighs, add them now and cook for 5–6 minutes. Add the tomato purée, bay leaves, lentils, and stock. If you are using chicken breast, add it now. Cover with a lid and simmer for 15 minutes until the lentils are tender.

To make the cucumber yogurt, put the yogurt in a small dish, add a good pinch of salt, and stir in the cucumber.

When the curry is cooked, season generously with salt and pepper (lentils tend to absorb a lot of seasoning, so don't be stingy). Transfer to bowls, scatter with cilantro, if using, and serve with a dollop of the cucumber yogurt. Serve with mango chutney and warm chapattis, rolled up, if desired.

Thai curry is a great flavor hit at the end of a busy day. Ready-made pastes make everything easier, but your curry will only be as good as your paste. Look for Thai brands, which are good but often very hot, or make your own and freeze it in small portions. Serve with steamed jasmine rice.

red curry with shrimp & pumpkin

If you remember, put the coconut milk in the refrigerator as soon as you buy it.

When you are ready to start cooking, scrape off the thick coconut cream that usually clings to the lid and put just the cream in a wok or large saucepan over medium heat. Add the curry paste and stir for 1–2 minutes until the paste smells fragrant, then add the sugar and cook for a further 2 minutes until sticky.

Pour in the rest of the coconut milk, add the lemon grass, pumpkin, and ⅓ –½ cup water to almost cover the pumpkin. Bring the contents of the wok to a gentle simmer and let bubble away gently for 10 minutes, or until the pumpkin is tender.

Add the sugar snap peas and cook for 2 minutes, then add the shrimp and cook for a further 2 minutes or until they turn pink. Remove from the heat and stir in the fish sauce. Transfer to bowls and sprinkle with the mint and chile. Taste and add more fish sauce if necessary. Serve with steamed jasmine rice.

14-oz. can coconut milk

2 tablespoons red curry paste

2 tablespoons palm sugar or natural cane sugar

1 lemon grass stalk, cut in half and bruised

14-oz. pumpkin or butternut squash, peeled, seeded, and cut into 1-inch chunks

4 oz. sugar snap peas, cut diagonally

6½ oz. uncooked tiger shrimp, shelled, deveined, and butterflied but tails intact

2 tablespoons Thai fish sauce

15 fresh mint leaves, finely shredded

1 large red chile, seeded and cut into thin strips

serves 4

This fiery curry from southern India is not for the fainthearted, although you can decrease the amounts of chile and curry powder to suit your palate. Serve with pickles as well as steamed basmati rice, if you like.

beef madras

1¾ lb. stewing beef, cut into large bite-size pieces

2 tablespoons safflower oil

1 dried bay leaf

1 cinnamon stick

3 cloves

4 cardamom pods, bruised

1 large onion, thinly sliced

3 garlic cloves, crushed

1 teaspoon finely grated fresh ginger

1 teaspoon ground turmeric

1 red chile, split in half lengthwise

2 teaspoons hot chili powder

2 teaspoons ground cumin

7 oz. canned chopped tomatoes

1¼ cups coconut milk, plus extra to drizzle

¼ teaspoon garam masala

sea salt and freshly ground black pepper

a small handful of chopped cilantro leaves, to garnish

marinade

5 tablespoons plain yogurt

3 tablespoons Madras curry powder

serves 4

To make the marinade, combine the yogurt and curry powder in a non-metallic bowl. Stir in the beef, season with salt, cover, and marinate in the fridge for 24 hours.

Heat the oil in a large, nonstick wok or skillet and add the bay leaf, cinnamon, cloves, and cardamom pods. Stir-fry for 1 minute, then add the onion. Stir-fry over medium heat for 4–5 minutes, then add the garlic, ginger, turmeric, red chile, chili powder, and cumin. Add the marinated beef (discarding the marinade) and stir-fry for 10–15 minutes over low heat.

Pour in the tomatoes and coconut milk and bring to a boil. Reduce the heat to low, cover tightly, and simmer gently for 1 hour, stirring occasionally. Stir in the garam masala 5 minutes before the end of cooking.

Check the seasoning. Drizzle with extra coconut milk and garnish with the cilantro. Serve immediately with steamed basmati rice and pickles, if you like.

This lightly spiced curry is the perfect comfort food. For the best results, make sure that you use very good-quality organic canned red kidney beans.

red kidney bean curry

Heat the butter and oil in a large, heavy-based saucepan and add the onion, cinnamon, bay leaves, garlic, and ginger and stir-fry for 4–5 minutes. Stir in the turmeric, ground coriander, cumin, garam masala, and chiles.

Add the kidney beans, tomato paste, and sufficient water to make a thick sauce. Bring to a boil and cook for 4–5 minutes, stirring often.

Season well, drizzle with yogurt, if desired, and garnish with cilantro.

1 tablespoon unsalted butter

2 tablespoons safflower oil

1 onion, finely chopped

1 cinnamon stick

2 dried bay leaves

3 garlic cloves, crushed

2 teaspoons finely grated fresh ginger

½ teaspoon ground turmeric

1 teaspoon ground coriander

2 teaspoons ground cumin

1 teaspoon garam masala

2 dried red chiles

1¼ cups canned red kidney beans, drained and rinsed

¼ cup tomato paste

sea salt and freshly ground black pepper

yogurt, to drizzle (optional)

freshly chopped cilantro leaves, to garnish

serves 4

The vibrant colors of Kerala, India's southernmost state, are all here on a plate. This deliciously creamy curry is made even richer with the addition of that irresistibly delicious snack, the cashew nut. Serve with either steamed or boiled basmati rice.

creamy vegetable curry

2 tablespoons vegetable oil

¾ cup large, unsalted cashew nuts

6 shallots, peeled and halved

1 teaspoon black mustard seeds

6–8 curry leaves

2 garlic cloves, chopped

1 tablespoon finely grated fresh ginger

1 teaspoon turmeric

4 large dried red chiles

1 small red bell pepper, thinly sliced

2 ripe tomatoes, quartered

8 very small new potatoes, halved

14-oz. can coconut milk

serves 4

Put the oil in a heavy-based saucepan set over medium heat. Add the cashew nuts and shallots and cook for 5 minutes, stirring often, until the cashews are just starting to brown. Add the mustard seeds and curry leaves and cook until the seeds start to pop. Add the garlic, ginger, turmeric, chiles, and red bell pepper to the pan and stir-fry for 2 minutes, until aromatic.

Add the tomatoes, potatoes, and coconut milk, partially cover the pan, and let simmer gently over low heat for about 20 minutes, or until the potatoes are cooked through. Spoon over basmati rice to serve, if liked.

Eggplant features in numerous iconic international meat-free dishes, including the spicy Middle Eastern dip baba ghanoush, Sicilian caponata, and the French classic ratatouille. This eggplant curry is tasty as well as colorful. Serve it with basmati rice if you like.

eggplant, tomato, & lentil curry

Heat the oil in a skillet set over high heat. When the oil is smoking hot, add the eggplant to the skillet and cook for 5 minutes, turning the pieces often so that they cook evenly. At first the eggplant will absorb the oil, but as it cooks to a dark and golden color, the oil will start to seep out back into the skillet. Remove the eggplant from the skillet at this point and not before.

Add the remaining oil, onion, garlic, and ginger to the skillet and cook for 5 minutes. Add the cherry tomatoes and cook for 1 minute, until they just soften and collapse, then remove them from the skillet before they break up too much. Set aside with the eggplant.

Add the curry leaves and cumin to the skillet and cook for a couple of minutes as the curry leaves pop and crackle. Add the chili powder, tomato paste, 2 cups water, and the lentils. Simmer for 15–20 minutes, until the lentils are tender but retain some bite. Stir in the eggplant and cherry tomatoes and cook the curry for a couple of minutes just to warm through. Stir in the cilantro and spoon over boiled or steamed basmati rice to serve, if liked.

3 tablespoons olive oil

1 large eggplant, cut into 8 pieces

1 red onion, chopped

2 garlic cloves, chopped

1 tablespoon finely chopped fresh ginger

8 oz. cherry tomatoes on the vine

6–8 curry leaves

1 teaspoon ground cumin

¼ teaspoon chili powder

1 tablespoon tomato paste

⅔ cup red lentils

1 handful of fresh cilantro, roughly chopped

serves 4

A mollee is a South Indian sauce, one of those dishes known wrongly in the rest of the world as a curry. It is mostly used for poaching fish, but is also delicious as a medium for reheating cooked meats or vegetables. The first step is to make the sauce: after that, you may add what you like.

fish mollee

1 lb. firm fish such as salmon, monkfish, or cod

1 tablespoon ground turmeric

1 teaspoon sea salt

½ cup unsalted butter

1 onion, chopped

1 garlic clove, crushed

2 small fresh green chiles, seeded if preferred, then chopped

1 inch fresh ginger, peeled and grated

12 cardamom pods, crushed

6 cloves, crushed

1 cinnamon stick

2 cups canned coconut milk

freshly squeezed lemon juice, to taste

freshly torn cilantro leaves, to serve

serves 4

Cut the fish into 1-inch strips. Mix the turmeric and salt on a plate, roll the fish in the mixture, and set aside for a few minutes.

Meanwhile, heat the butter in a flameproof casserole dish or large saucepan. Add the onion, garlic, chiles, ginger, cardamom, cloves, and cinnamon stick and sauté until the onion is softened and translucent.

Add the coconut milk, heat until simmering, and cook until the mixture is quite thick. Add the fish to the casserole dish, then spoon the sauce over the top, making sure the fish is well covered. Cook for 10 minutes, until the fish is opaque all the way through. Serve sprinkled with lemon juice and cilantro.

The orange of the butternut squash contrasted with the green of the spinach makes this a particularly colorful dish. Serve with steamed basmati rice and other curry dishes or with naan bread.

spicy butternut & chicken curry

Heat the oil in a nonstick skillet or wok, add the mustard seeds, and stir-fry until they pop. Add half the butternut squash or pumpkin and all of the onions and stir-fry gently until the onions are softened and translucent. Add the garlic, ginger, salt, and pepper and stir-fry for 1 minute. Add the turmeric and stir-fry for 1 minute more.

Add the chicken, stir-fry until sealed on all sides, then add the tomatoes and remaining butternut. Bring to a boil, then reduce the heat, and simmer, covered, for about 20 minutes, or until tender.

Add the cream, bring to a boil and simmer, stirring, until thickened—the cream will first boil with large bubbles, then small. Stop at this point or the cream will curdle. Add the spinach and garam masala, cover with a lid, and steam for 2 minutes until the leaves collapse, then stir into the rest of the ingredients. Serve with steamed basmati rice and other curry dishes or with naan bread.

2 tablespoons safflower or peanut oil

1 tablespoon mustard seeds

1 lb. butternut squash or pumpkin, peeled, seeded, and cut into 1-inch cubes

2 onions, thinly sliced

2 garlic cloves, crushed

1 inch fresh ginger, peeled and grated (optional)

a pinch of ground turmeric

4 chicken breasts, skinless and boneless, cut into 1-inch slices

1 lb. tomatoes, peeled and coarsely chopped

1 cup heavy cream

1 large package of fresh spinach, about 1 lb.

a pinch of garam masala

sea salt and freshly ground black pepper

serves 4

bakes & gratins

This absolutely delicious dish, inspired by paella, never fails to impress and delight, and because it's all cooked in the oven, it really couldn't be easier.

oven-roasted spicy macaroni

Preheat the oven to 400°F.

Put the cherry tomatoes into the roasting pan and sprinkle with the onion, garlic, and oil. Roast in the preheated oven for about 20 minutes until the tomatoes are soft.

Remove from the oven and add the macaroni, chicken, chorizo, rosemary, stock, saffron, salt, and pepper. Mix well and return it to the oven to bake for 30 minutes.

Add the shrimp and bake for a further 5 minutes until the pasta and chicken are cooked. Sprinkle with basil and serve.

1 pint cherry tomatoes

1 red onion, finely chopped

2 garlic cloves, finely chopped

2 tablespoons olive oil

10 oz. small macaroni, about 3 cups

4 boneless, skinless chicken thighs, quartered crosswise

8 oz. chorizo, thickly sliced

2 teaspoons freshly chopped rosemary

1 quart chicken stock

a pinch of saffron threads

8 large, uncooked shrimp

sea salt and freshly ground black pepper

a handful of basil leaves, torn, to serve

serves 4

This very versatile dish, served on a base of thyme and lemon, can be prepared in advance. It then needs only to be roasted and basted for an effortless supper. If you wish, you can serve it with a tomato or herb sauce and roast fennel.

roast cod cutlets

6 cod cutlets, 8 oz. each for an entrée, 7 oz. as an appetizer

about 2 tablespoons unsalted butter

freshly grated nutmeg

6 lemon slices

2 large potatoes, parboiled in salted water and cut into walnut-size pieces

sea salt and freshly ground black pepper

base of thyme & lemon

1 stick plus 5 tablespoons unsalted butter

2 onions, chopped

2 garlic cloves, crushed

1 teaspoon fresh lemon thyme leaves

6 peppercorns

2 bay leaves

serves 6

Preheat the oven to 375°F.

Season the cutlets with salt and pepper.

To make the base of thyme and lemon, heat the butter in a skillet, add the onions, garlic, thyme, peppercorns, and bay leaves, and cook gently until softened but not browned.

Spread the mixture in a roasting pan. Put the cutlets on top, with about 1 teaspoon of the butter on each piece. Add the nutmeg and lemon slices. Tuck the potato pieces around. Roast in the preheated oven for 35 minutes, basting once with the juices from the lemon slices.

Serve as it is, or with a tomato or herb sauce and roast fennel.

A mixture of very finely chopped vegetables forms the basis of this dish. It can be served either very hot straight from the oven or left until cold, which is delicious in summer. In winter, you could use fresh herrings instead of sardines. Eat it with bread to mop up the juices.

baked sardines

Preheat the oven to 375°F.

Heat 3 tablespoons of the oil in a skillet, add the bell pepper, onions, and garlic and cook gently until softened but not colored, 8–10 minutes. Add the tomatoes, paprika, saffron, cumin, and bay leaves and cook for a further 5–8 minutes (add a little water if the mixture sticks to the skillet) until completely cooked. Season with salt and pepper and fold in the parsley.

Put the sardine fillets on a plate, skin side down, and sprinkle with a little salt and pepper.

Arrange one-third of the fillets, skin side up, in an ovenproof dish. Cover with one-third of the cooked mixture. Repeat twice more—when adding the last layer, let the silver sardine skin peek through. Grind over a little more pepper and spoon over the rest of the oil.

Bake in the preheated oven for 15–20 minutes until sizzling. Sprinkle with parsley leaves, then serve.

½ cup extra virgin olive oil

1 red bell pepper, seeded and finely chopped

2 medium onions, finely chopped

3 garlic cloves, crushed

2 large tomatoes, peeled, seeded, and cut into 1-inch cubes

1 teaspoon hot paprika

a pinch of saffron

¼ teaspoon ground cumin

2 bay leaves

2 tablespoons freshly chopped flatleaf parsley, plus extra leaves to serve

9–12 fresh sardine fillets (depending on the size of the dish)

sea salt and freshly ground black pepper

serves 4–6

This Middle Eastern dish supposedly got its name because the priest (the imam) found it so delicious that he swooned. Some stories tell that he really fainted because he was horrified at the amount of oil used to cook it. This, of course, is the secret of the dish—the eggplant must be cooked well, with large quantities of oil.

imam bayildi

4 large eggplant,
with long stalks if possible,
halved lengthwise

¾ cup extra virgin olive oil

1 lb. onions, halved and
very thinly sliced

4 garlic cloves, crushed

1½ lb. Italian plum tomatoes,
peeled, seeded, and finely
chopped

leaves from 15 sprigs of
flatleaf parsley

leaves from 12 sprigs of
marjoram

2 teaspoons sugar

1 small lemon, thinly sliced

sea salt and freshly ground
black pepper

serves 4–8

Preheat the oven to 400°F.

Cut a line ¼ inch in from the edges of the eggplant halves, then score the flesh inside with a criss-cross pattern. Rub plenty of oil all over the eggplant and season with a little salt. Arrange in a single layer in an ovenproof dish. Cook in the preheated oven for about 30 minutes or until the flesh has just softened.

Heat ⅓ cup of the oil in a heavy skillet, add the onions and garlic, cover with a lid, and cook over low heat until soft. Increase the heat and add the tomatoes. Cook until the juices from the tomatoes have reduced a little, then add salt and pepper to taste. Reserve a few parsley leaves for serving, then chop the remainder together with the marjoram. Add to the onion and tomato mixture, then add the sugar.

Scoop some of the central flesh out of the eggplant, leaving a shell around the outside to hold the base in shape. Chop the scooped-out flesh and add to the tomato mixture. Pile the mixture into the eggplant shells and sprinkle with pepper. Arrange the lemon slices on top. Trail more oil generously over the top, then sprinkle with ¼ cup water.

Cover with foil and bake for 30–40 minutes until meltingly soft. Remove the foil about 10 minutes before the end. Serve, sprinkled with any remaining oil and the reserved parsley.

Cream and potatoes, mingling in the heat of the oven, are almost all you'll find in this well-loved dish. Serve on its own, with mixed salad greens, or as a partner for a dish of roast meat or poultry.

creamy potato gratin

Preheat the oven to 350°F.

Put the potatoes in a large saucepan with the milk and bay leaf. Bring to a boil, then lower the heat, add a pinch of salt, and simmer gently until partially cooked, 5–10 minutes.

Drain the potatoes. When cool enough to handle (but still hot), slice into rounds about ⅛ inch thick.

Spread the butter in the bottom of a baking dish. Arrange half the potato slices in the dish and sprinkle with salt. Put the remaining potato on top and sprinkle with more salt. Pour in the cream and sprinkle with the grated nutmeg.

Bake in the preheated oven until golden and the cream is almost absorbed, but not completely, about 45 minutes. Serve hot, on its own, or with mixed salad greens, or with roast meat or poultry.

4½ lb. boiling potatoes, cut in half if large

2 quarts whole milk

1 fresh bay leaf

2 tablespoons unsalted butter

2 cups whipping cream

a pinch of freshly grated nutmeg

sea salt

serves 4–6

This is a hearty hotpot packed with fall vegetables and rich with smoky paprika. Great northern beans are large and white, resembling lima beans in shape but with a distinctive, delicate flavor. Serve with warm bread to dip in the sauce.

smoky hotpot

2 tablespoons olive oil

1 large onion, chopped

2 garlic cloves, chopped

2 teaspoons smoked paprika

1 celery rib, chopped

1 carrot, chopped

2 medium waxy potatoes, cut into 1-inch dice

1 red bell pepper, chopped

2 cups vegetable stock

7 oz. canned great northern or lima beans, drained and rinsed

sea salt and freshly ground black pepper

crusty bread, to serve

serves 4

Put the oil in a saucepan set over medium heat. Add the onion and cook for 4–5 minutes until softened. Add the garlic and paprika to the pan and stir-fry for 2 minutes. Add the celery, carrot, potatoes, and bell pepper and cook for 2 minutes, stirring constantly to coat the vegetables in the flavored oil.

Add the stock and beans and bring to a boil. Reduce the heat and partially cover the pan with a lid. Let simmer for 40 minutes, stirring often, until all the vegetables are cooked. Season to taste and serve with crusty bread.

A few chickpeas are all that are needed to turn an unassuming tray of early-fall roasted vegetables into a great dinner. Serve with some spicy couscous to soak up the tasty juices.

roasted vegetables & chickpeas

Preheat the oven to 350°F.

Put the mushrooms, tomatoes, red and yellow bell peppers, onion, fennel, and garlic in a large roasting pan. Sprinkle the salt evenly over the vegetables and drizzle with the oil. Roast in the preheated oven for 1 hour.

Remove the pan from the oven and turn the vegetables. Add the chickpeas and thyme sprigs. Return the pan to the oven and roast for a further 30 minutes, until the edges of the vegetables are just starting to blacken.

To serve, spoon spiced couscous (if using) onto serving plates and top with the roasted vegetables and chickpeas.

12 small mushrooms

2 ripe tomatoes, halved

1 red bell pepper, cut into strips

1 yellow bell pepper, cut into strips

1 red onion, cut into wedges

1 small fennel bulb, sliced into thin wedges

1 garlic bulb, broken into cloves but left unpeeled

2 teaspoons sea salt

2 tablespoons olive oil

14-oz. can chickpeas, drained and rinsed

2 fresh thyme or rosemary sprigs

serves 4

The Queensland Blue pumpkin is for some the best pumpkin of all. A squashed turban shape, it is very dense and firm, with a beautiful dark blue-green-gray skin and brilliant orange flesh. Don't worry if you can't find this variety—there are many others that will fit the bill. Choose one large pumpkin or several smaller ones.

baked stuffed pumpkin

1 large pumpkin, about 6 lb., or 6 small pumpkins

olive oil, for brushing

filling

1–2 carrots, sliced

2 tablespoons olive oil

4 slices bacon, chopped

1–2 onions, finely sliced

3 garlic cloves, crushed

1 inch fresh ginger, peeled and finely chopped

leaves from 3–4 sprigs of oregano or thyme, chopped

2 cups ground beef

2 teaspoons tomato paste

1–2 fresh red chiles, halved, seeded, and chopped

1 cup cooked white rice

leaves from 1 large bunch of fresh flatleaf parsley, chopped

sea salt and freshly ground black pepper

serves 6–8

Preheat the oven to 400°F.

Using a small, sharp knife, cut a "plug" out of the top of the pumpkin, including the stalk, if any, and reserve. Scoop out and discard all the seeds and fibers. Brush the inside of the pumpkin with oil.

Parboil the carrots in boiling salted water until almost cooked. Drain and set aside.

Put the oil in a nonstick skillet, add the bacon, and stir-fry until crisp. Remove with a slotted spoon and drain on paper towels.

Add the onions to the skillet and sauté until softened and translucent. Add the garlic and ginger and stir-fry until the onion is golden. Add the oregano or thyme and the beef and stir-fry until the meat is browned. Stir in the tomato paste and chiles. Add the carrots, bacon, and rice and stir-fry until hot—the mixture should be fairly stiff.

Mix in the parsley then use the mixture to stuff the pumpkin—the mixture is already cooked, so it won't expand. Put the lid on top and and envelop the bottom of the pumpkin in a "basin" of foil. Bake in the preheated oven for 45–60 minutes or until the pumpkin is tender. Test with the point of a skewer—the time will depend on the pumpkin variety and its size.

Baking sliced potatoes and mushrooms in layers lets the potatoes absorb the juices and earthy flavor of the mushrooms. Try to use the darkest mushrooms you can find—they will have the best taste. You can always mix fresh ones with reconstituted dried mushrooms for a more intense flavor.

potato & mushroom gratin

Preheat the oven to 350°F.

Peel the potatoes and slice thickly, putting them in a bowl of cold water as you go to stop them from browning. Trim the mushrooms and slice thickly. Put half the potatoes in a layer in the bottom of a well-buttered ovenproof dish, sprinkle with oil, and cover with half the mushrooms.

Put the bread crumbs, Parmesan, parsley, and some salt and pepper in a bowl and mix well. Spread half this mixture over the mushrooms, then sprinkle with more oil. Cover with a second layer of the potatoes, then the remaining mushrooms. Finally, sprinkle with the remaining bread crumb mixture and more oil.

Cover with foil and bake in the preheated oven for 30 minutes. Uncover and cook for a further 30 minutes until the potatoes are tender and the top is golden brown.

2 lb. medium potatoes

1½ lb. flavorsome mushrooms such as portobello (or use fresh wild mushrooms)

extra virgin olive oil, for sprinkling

3½ cups stale (not dry) white bread crumbs

¼ cup freshly grated Parmesan cheese

¼ cup chopped flatleaf parsley

sea salt and freshly ground black pepper

serves 4

casseroles & stews

In its native Basque region of Spain, this stew is called marmitako. The name comes from the French word *marmite* —a tall, straight-sided stewpot made from copper, iron, or earthenware. The fishermen used to make this stew on board their boats, using tuna from the Bay of Biscay, and mopping up the soupy juices with lots of delicious fried bread.

tuna & potato stew

Halve and seed the red, yellow, and green bell peppers and cut the flesh into ½-inch chunks.

Heat the oil in a flameproof casserole dish, add the onion, garlic, and peppers and sauté over low heat until softened but not colored, 12–15 minutes. Increase the heat and stir in the tomatoes and their juice. When the mixture starts to thicken, add the paprika, bay leaf, salt, and pepper.

Stir in the potatoes and 1¾ cups boiling water and simmer gently for about 15 minutes until the potatoes are cooked.

Season the pieces of tuna 10 minutes before cooking. Add the tuna to the casserole dish and after about 30 seconds, when the underside turns pale, turn the pieces over and turn off the heat. Leave for 5 minutes. Sprinkle with parsley. Serve with triangles of fried bread, if you wish.

1 small red bell pepper

1 small yellow bell pepper

1 small green bell pepper

3 tablespoons extra virgin olive oil

1 large onion, finely chopped

2 garlic cloves, finely chopped

5 tomatoes, peeled, seeded, and chopped (reserve any juices)

½ teaspoon sweet paprika

1 bay leaf

1 lb. potatoes, peeled and cut into ½-inch slices

2 slices of fresh tuna, 1 lb. each, cut into 12 chunky pieces

2 tablespoons flatleaf parsley leaves, torn

sea salt and freshly ground black pepper

fried bread, cut into triangles, to serve (optional)

serves 4–6

This easy, stress-free recipe makes a fantastic meal. Don't forget to provide a few empty dishes for discarded shells and some bowls of warm water for washing fingers. Serve with plenty of warm crusty bread.

easy fish stew

⅓ cup olive oil

3 garlic cloves, chopped

2 onions, chopped

2 leeks, trimmed and sliced

3 celery ribs, sliced

1 fennel bulb, trimmed and sliced

1 tablespoon all-purpose flour

1 bay leaf

a sprig of thyme

a generous pinch of saffron threads

3 x 14-oz. cans chopped tomatoes

2 quarts fish stock

2 lb. monkfish tail, cut into 8 pieces

1 lb. mussels in shells, scrubbed

8 scallops

8 uncooked shrimp, shell on

a bunch of flatleaf parsley, chopped

sea salt and freshly ground black pepper

serves 8

Heat the oil in a large saucepan and add the garlic, onions, leeks, celery, and fennel. Cook over low to medium heat for 10 minutes until soft. Sprinkle in the flour and stir well. Add the bay leaf, thyme, saffron, tomatoes, fish stock, and salt and pepper to taste. Bring to a boil, then simmer for 25 minutes.

Add the monkfish, mussels, scallops, and shrimp, cover with a lid, and simmer very gently for 6 minutes. Remove from the heat and set aside, with the lid on, for 4 minutes. Add the parsley and serve with warm crusty bread. Take care not to eat the mussels that haven't fully opened.

Chicken with rice is a universal favorite, and it is always a good bet when entertaining large numbers or mixed ages. The inspiration came from paella, though this is baked, so you can put it in the oven and forget about it, almost, until serving time. The dish tastes better if the ingredients aren't packed in too deeply.

chicken, sausage, & rice

Preheat the oven to 400°F.

Tie the bay leaf, thyme, and parsley together with kitchen string.

Heat the oil in a large ovenproof pan with a lid. Add the chicken pieces skin side down and cook on high heat until browned, 3–5 minutes. Repeat on the other side. Work in batches if all the pieces will not fit comfortably in the pan. Transfer the browned chicken to a plate and season with salt and pepper.

Add the sausages to the pan and cook until browned. Remove and cut into 3–4 pieces, depending on their size. Remove and set aside.

Add the onion, bell pepper, and celery and cook on high heat until they begin to brown and smell aromatic, 2–3 minutes. Add the garlic, red pepper flakes, and some salt and pepper and cook for 1 minute more.

Stir in the rice until all the grains are coated. Add the wine, stock, tomatoes, and some salt and mix well. Add the bunch of herbs, the chicken, and sausage.

Cover the pan and bake in the preheated oven until the rice is cooked, about 30 minutes. After 20 minutes, add the peas on top and a little bit of water if the liquid has almost completely evaporated. Cook for 10 minutes more. Remove from the oven and set aside, covered, for 10 minutes. Remove the bunch of herbs and fluff up the rice to mix in the peas. Serve hot.

1 bay leaf

a few sprigs of thyme and parsley

1 tablespoon extra virgin olive oil

8 chicken thighs, trimmed

6 pure pork sausages

1 onion, chopped

1 red bell pepper, chopped

2 celery ribs, chopped

3 garlic cloves, finely chopped

¼–½ teaspoon hot red pepper flakes, or more to taste

2 cups calasparra (paella) rice

½ cup dry wine, red or white

1¼ cups fresh unsalted chicken stock

14 oz. canned chopped tomatoes

2 cups peas, about 10 oz., fresh or frozen and thawed

sea salt and freshly ground black pepper

serves 4–6

These little spring leeks are so small that they are easily confused with scallions. The green tips are soft and, although people might not want to eat them, they do give a more leeky flavor to the dish if left on. The dish could also be made with aromatic spices like paprika and cumin. It works well alongside couscous mixed with pine nuts.

lemony chicken with leeks

½ cup all-purpose flour

1 organic spring chicken, about 3½ lb., cut into 10 pieces

½ cup light olive oil

12 baby leeks

3 garlic cloves, chopped

1 unwaxed lemon, thickly sliced

½ cup white wine

½ cup freshly squeezed lemon juice

½ cup chicken stock

1 tablespoon light soy sauce

sea salt and freshly ground black pepper

serves 4

Season the flour with salt and pepper and put it in a clean plastic bag. Add half the chicken pieces and shake to coat them in the seasoned flour. Repeat with the remaining chicken pieces. Set aside until needed.

Heat the oil in a large skillet over medium-high heat. Add the leeks and stir-fry for 4 minutes, until softened and silky. Remove the leeks from the skillet and set aside. Add half of the chicken to the skillet and cook in batches for 4–5 minutes, turning each piece often, until golden brown all over. Transfer the browned chicken to a plate and repeat to cook the remaining chicken.

Pour off all but 1 tablespoon of oil from the skillet, leaving any sediment behind. Add the garlic and lemon and cook for 1 minute, stirring well to combine with any of the cooked-on bits from the bottom of the skillet. Add the wine and let sizzle for 1 minute, then add the lemon juice, chicken stock, and soy sauce and bring to a boil. Return the chicken to the pan and cook for 20 minutes. Turn each piece of chicken, then put the leeks on top of the chicken. Cover the pan with cooking foil and cook for a further 20 minutes, until the chicken is cooked through. Stir to combine the chicken and any of the cooking juices evenly with the leeks. Serve with couscous, if you wish.

The red rice from the Camargue area of southern France used in this dish is justly famous. It takes over twice the usual time to cook, but is good served with hearty wine and other intense tastes, as in this easy chicken dish.

camargue chicken

Pat the chicken breasts dry with paper towels and cut 2 slashes on top of each.

Heat half the butter and all the oil in a large flameproof casserole dish and brown the chicken, skin side first, until golden. Remove from the pan and set aside.

Add the garlic and rice to the pan and stir over high heat for 1 minute. Pour in the chicken stock and 1¼ cups boiling water. Add the white part of the leeks, and some salt and pepper. Cover the pan and cook over low heat for 3 minutes. Uncover, then add the chicken pieces, pushing them into the rice. Add the white wine and put the bacon on top.

Increase the heat slightly. Cover the pan again and cook for a further 10–12 minutes, then add the tarragon vinegar, the fresh tarragon, if using, and the green part of the leeks. Cook for a final 5 minutes, uncover the pan, and add the remaining butter, tilting the pan to mix. Serve hot with the same wine used in cooking.

* If red rice is unavailable, you could substitute wild rice, but presoak it for 2 hours in hot (not boiling) water to shorten the cooking time. Drain, then proceed as above.

4 boneless chicken breasts, preferably free range, or 4 chicken quarters

2 tablespoons salted butter

¼ cup virgin olive oil

2 garlic cloves, chopped

1¼ cups Camargue red rice *

2 cups hot chicken stock

3 leeks, white parts sliced into 2-inch chunks, green tops finely sliced

½ cup robust white wine

6 slices smoked bacon or pancetta, whole or cut into strips

2 tablespoons tarragon vinegar

30–40 fresh tarragon leaves (optional)

sea salt and freshly ground black pepper

serves 4

This is one of the easiest supper dishes imaginable. It takes less time to cook than a ready meal and is much more delicious. You can use any dry white wine, but Viognier, an exotic, slightly scented grape variety, is particularly good. Unoaked or lightly oaked Chardonnay will also work well. Steamed asparagus tips are a good accompaniment.

chicken with white wine

1 tablespoon olive oil

3½ oz. pancetta or lean bacon, chopped

2 skinless, boneless chicken breasts, cut into thin slices

1 small onion, very finely chopped

⅔ cup full-bodied dry white wine, such as Viognier

1 cup green peas, fresh or frozen and thawed

2 tablespoons finely chopped fresh tarragon leaves

about 4 generous tablespoons sour cream or crème fraîche

freshly ground black pepper

serves 2

Heat the oil in a large skillet, then add the pancetta or bacon. Sauté for a couple of minutes until the fat starts to run. Add the chicken slices and sauté, stirring occasionally, until lightly golden, 4–5 minutes.

Add the onion to the pan and sauté for 1–2 minutes. Add the wine and peas and cook until the wine has reduced by about two-thirds. Reduce the heat and stir in the tarragon, sour cream or crème fraîche, and pepper, to taste. Heat gently until almost bubbling.

Remove the pan from the heat. Transfer the chicken to warm plates, spoon over the sauce, and serve immediately with steamed asparagus tips, if you wish.

Typically, this traditional French dish is thickened and enriched with butter but here extra virgin olive oil has been used instead. Good-quality red wine vinegar is essential. Cheap vinegar is far too astringent for this dish and will produce a harsh and unpleasant sauce—a far cry from the mouthwatering result you should get.

poulet sauté au vinaigre

Heat 3 tablespoons of the oil in a large skillet. Season the chicken all over and cook for 3–4 minutes on each side, or until golden. Add the tomatoes and garlic to the skillet. Cook for 10–15 minutes, squashing the tomatoes down with the back of a spoon, until they are thick and sticky and have lost all their moisture.

Pour in the red wine vinegar and let it bubble for 10–15 minutes, until the liquid has almost evaporated. Pour in the stock, and cook for a further 15 minutes or so, until reduced by half.

Stir in the remaining oil and parsley and serve with salad greens.

6 tablespoons extra virgin olive oil

a 4½-lb. chicken, cut into 8 pieces

1 lb. very ripe cherry tomatoes

2 garlic cloves, crushed

¾ cup good-quality red wine vinegar

1¼ cups chicken stock

a small bunch of fresh flatleaf parsley, chopped

sea salt and freshly ground black pepper

salad greens, to serve

serves 4–6

The bacon adds a special intensity to the flavor of this easy-to-make dish. Serve with some wild rice on the side to mop up the lovely sauce.

chicken & bacon pot

1 tablespoon olive oil

10 oz. thick bacon, diced

8 oz. button mushrooms

4 chicken breasts

1 garlic clove, crushed

2 shallots, diced

⅓ cup all-purpose flour

2 cups chicken stock

1 cup white wine

1 bay leaf

a handful of fresh flatleaf parsley, chopped

sea salt and freshly ground black pepper

serves 4

Preheat the oven to 350°F.

Heat the oil in a flameproof casserole dish, add the bacon and mushrooms, and cook over medium heat until golden. Transfer to a plate.

Put the chicken breasts in the casserole dish and quickly brown on both sides. Set aside with the bacon.

Sauté the garlic and shallots over low heat in the same dish for 5 minutes. Add the flour and mix well. Remove the dish from the heat, slowly pour in the stock and wine, and stir until smooth. Return to the heat and bring to a boil, stirring constantly. Mix in the bacon and mushrooms, then add the chicken breasts, bay leaf, and seasoning. Cover and cook in the oven for 30 minutes. Add the parsley just before serving with an accompaniment of wild rice.

Moroccan cuisine often marries sweet and savory ingredients to surprisingly good effect, as in this richly flavored sauce. Serve with either bulgur wheat or couscous mixed with parsley and lemon zest and juice.

moroccan honey & lemon chicken

Lightly season the chicken breasts, then heat 1 tablespoon of the honey in a nonstick sauté pan. Add the chicken and the garlic and sauté the chicken breasts for 1 minute on each side over medium heat until caramelized, but watch carefully to ensure that the honey doesn't burn.

Stir the tomatoes into the pan and add the remaining honey, the cinnamon, lemon zest, and juice. Bring to a simmer and cook, uncovered, for 15 minutes.

Scatter the toasted almonds over the chicken and sauce. Serve with bulgur wheat or couscous.

4 skinless and boneless chicken breasts, about 4 oz. each

3 tablespoons clear honey

2 garlic cloves, sliced

14 oz. canned chopped tomatoes

½ teaspoon ground cinnamon

grated zest and freshly squeezed juice of ½ unwaxed lemon

sea salt and freshly ground black pepper

2 tablespoons toasted slivered almonds, to garnish

serves 4

Comfort food at its best, this chicken and barley dish is quick and easy to make, as well as a joy to eat. Choose a selection of your favorite vegetables to serve on the side—baby carrots sprinkled with fresh tarragon make a colorful accompaniment.

chicken & barley supper

2 tablespoons whole-wheat flour

1 lb. skinless, boneless chicken breasts, cut into cubes

3½ oz. lean bacon slices, cut into strips

2 medium onions, chopped

2 carrots, sliced

2 celery ribs, chopped

3–4 cups white wine or chicken stock

3 tablespoons pearl barley, rinsed

1 tablespoon mixed chopped fresh herbs, such as flatleaf parsley, rosemary, basil, and thyme

freshly ground black pepper

chopped flatleaf parsley, to serve

serves 4

Season the flour with pepper, then toss the chicken cubes in the flour. Heat a large nonstick sauté pan or saucepan, add the bacon, and dry-fry for 5 minutes, stirring frequently, until the fat starts to run. Add the chicken and sauté for 5–8 minutes, turning frequently, until the chicken is sealed all over. Remove the chicken and bacon from the pan with a slotted spoon and set aside.

Add the onion, carrots, celery, and ¼ cup of the wine or stock to the pan and sauté for 5–8 minutes, until the vegetables are softened. Add the pearl barley, herbs, and 2½ cups of the wine or stock. Bring to a boil, then cover, reduce the heat, and simmer for 1 hour. Add more wine or stock as it is absorbed.

Return the chicken and bacon to the pan and continue to simmer for a further 30 minutes, or until the pearl barley and chicken are tender. Stir occasionally during cooking, adding a little more wine or stock, if necessary. Serve, sprinkled with chopped parsley and accompanied by a selection of your favorite vegetables.

A huge, colorful stew is very festive and inviting, and this one, based on a traditional Portuguese recipe, makes a nice change from the standard repertoire. For best results, use imported Portuguese piri piri sauce. But beware if you've never tried it before—piri piri is very hot, and the heat varies from one brand to another. Serve with couscous.

lamb stew with piri piri

Preheat the oven to 375°F.

To make the marinade, put the onion, vinegar, paprika, garlic, cilantro, parsley, and salt in a large non-metallic dish. Mix well. Add the lamb and turn to coat thoroughly. Cover with plastic wrap and refrigerate for at least 3 hours or overnight.

Heat the oil in a large ovenproof saucepan with a lid. When hot, add the lamb and all the marinade. Sprinkle with the flour and stir to coat well. Cook to sear the meat, 3–5 minutes, then stir in 1 cup water. Add the potatoes, carrots, some salt, and piri piri and mix well. Cover and transfer to the preheated oven for 50 minutes.

Add the zucchini and red bell pepper and continue cooking for another 40 minutes. Remove from the oven and stir in the chickpeas. Add salt and pepper to taste, and more piri piri if you like. Serve hot, with couscous on the side.

2¼ lb. boneless lamb, cubed

2 tablespoons extra virgin olive oil

1½ tablespoons all-purpose flour

1 lb. potatoes, peeled and cut into large chunks

1 lb. carrots, cut into large pieces

1–2 teaspoons piri piri sauce

1½ lb. zucchini, cut into thick rounds

1 red bell pepper, seeded and cut into pieces

14 oz. canned unsalted chickpeas, drained and rinsed

sea salt and freshly ground black pepper

marinade

1 onion, chopped

⅓ cup sherry vinegar

1½ teaspoons sweet smoked Spanish paprika

4 garlic cloves, sliced

a large handful of fresh cilantro, chopped

a large handful of fresh flatleaf parsley, chopped

1 tablespoon sea salt

serves 6

1 tablespoon safflower oil

1½ lb. boneless rib lamb chops, cubed

1 lb. boneless loin lamb chops, each one cut into several pieces

1 tablespoon all-purpose flour

2 vine-ripened tomatoes, peeled, seeded, and chopped

2 garlic cloves, crushed

2¾ cups fresh lamb or chicken stock

1 fresh bay leaf

a sprig of thyme

4 baby carrots, cut into 1-inch pieces

8 oz. baby leeks, cut into 2-inch lengths

8 oz. baby turnips

8 oz. sugar snap peas

a handful of flatleaf parsley, chopped

sea salt and freshly ground black pepper

serves 4

Herald in the spring with this lovely lamb stew with vegetables—it's tasty, filling, and straightforward to make. Serve with boiled baby new potatoes.

spring lamb stew

Heat the oil in a large casserole dish, add the lamb, and brown the pieces on all sides, in batches if necessary. When all the lamb has been browned, return it all to the pan, lower the heat slightly, and stir in a pinch of salt and the flour. Cook, stirring to coat evenly, for 1 minute.

Add the tomatoes and garlic. Stir in the stock, bay leaf, and thyme. Bring to a boil and skim off any foam that rises to the surface. Reduce the heat, then cover and simmer gently for 40 minutes.

Add the carrots, leeks, and turnips and cook for 25 minutes more. Taste and adjust the seasoning with salt and pepper.

Add the peas and cook for 7 minutes. Sprinkle with the parsley and serve immediately.

A fantastic dish that can be made in advance and finished off on the day: this makes your life easier and also improves the flavor of the dish. All the vegetables can be altered to suit your taste: try leeks, cauliflower, and broccoli florets, asparagus, parsnips, turnips, pumpkin, or sweet potatoes— the list is endless. Serve with garlic bread.

lamb navarin

Trim any excess fat from the lamb. Heat the oil in a large flameproof casserole dish or saucepan, add the lamb, and cook briefly until browned all over. Depending on the size of the pan, you may have to do this in batches.

Return all the meat to the pan, sprinkle with a fine dusting of flour, mix well, and repeat until all the flour has been incorporated. Add the stock, tomatoes, tomato paste, wine, herbs, paprika, garlic, and shallots. Mix well and bring to a boil. Reduce the heat and simmer gently for 1 hour, stirring from time to time. Add salt and pepper to taste. (If making in advance, prepare up to this point, let cool, then chill overnight.)

Add the carrots, potatoes, and celery and cook for 15 minutes. Add the runner beans and curly kale or greens and stir gently. Cover with a lid and cook for a further 5 minutes. Serve with garlic bread.

4 lb. boneless leg or shoulder of lamb, cubed

3 tablespoons olive oil

3 tablespoons all-purpose flour

1 quart vegetable stock

2 x 14-oz. cans chopped tomatoes

1 tablespoon tomato paste

⅔ cup red wine

2 bay leaves

2 sprigs of marjoram

½ teaspoon smoked paprika

2 garlic cloves, crushed and chopped

8 shallots, finely chopped

10 oz. baby carrots, scrubbed

10 oz. new potatoes

3 celery ribs, cut into chunks

4 oz. runner beans, chopped

2 oz. curly kale or other greens, coarsely chopped

sea salt and freshly ground black pepper

serves 8

This Greek-style dish is very simple but surprisingly effective, considering how few ingredients there are, so make sure you adjust the seasoning carefully, as it makes such a difference. Trim the stem end only of the okra, to discourage the sticky liquid from oozing out. Serve with new potatoes sprinkled with freshly chopped flatleaf parsley.

braised lamb with okra

3 tablespoons olive oil

4 lamb steaks, about 2 lb., cut from the leg and deboned

1 small onion, sliced

2 garlic cloves, crushed

4 tomatoes, peeled and seeded

8 oz. okra, trimmed

sea salt and freshly ground black pepper

serves 4

Preheat the oven to 350°F.

Heat the oil in a large, wide, shallow, flameproof casserole dish or saucepan. Season the meat with salt and pepper, add to the pan, and brown the pieces all over. Remove the meat with a slotted spoon, put on a plate, and set aside in a warm place.

Add the onion and garlic to the pan and cook until softened and lightly browned. Add the tomatoes and simmer to a pulp.

Return the lamb to the pan, turn to coat, taste and adjust the seasoning, and cover with a lid. Bring to a boil on top of the stove, then transfer to the preheated oven and simmer for 20 minutes.

Add the okra, cover, and simmer for a further 20 minutes, removing the lid for the last 10 minutes of cooking time, to let the liquid reduce enough to just coat the meat without becoming oily. Serve with new potatoes, sprinkled with freshly chopped parsley.

This version of a daube, a classic French dish made with beef and red wine, contains walnut halves and Cognac—heart-warming, welcoming, and grand. Use good-quality extra virgin olive oil. Serve hot—either on its own, or with accompaniments such as pasta, mashed potatoes, or rice.

boeuf en daube

Cut the beef into 2-inch squares. Heat the oil in a large flameproof casserole dish and gently sauté the garlic, bacon, carrots, and onions for about 4–5 minutes or until aromatic. Remove from the casserole dish. Put a layer of meat in the bottom of the casserole dish, then add half the fried vegetable mixture and a second layer of meat. Add the remaining vegetable mixture, the tomatoes, orange zest, herbs, and walnuts.

Put the wine into a small saucepan and bring to a boil. Add the Cognac or brandy and warm for a few seconds, shaking the pan a little, to let the alcohol cook away. Pour the hot liquids over the meat with just enough stock so that it's barely covered.

Heat the casserole until simmering, then cover with foil and a lid and simmer gently for 2 hours or until the meat is fork-tender and the juices rich and sticky.

Sprinkle with the parsley. Serve the casserole on its own, or with pasta, mashed potatoes, or rice.

2 lb. beef, such as shoulder or topside, cut into ½-inch thick slices

¼ cup extra virgin olive oil

4 garlic cloves, sliced

1 cup thick-cut unsmoked bacon, cut into small dice, or bacon lardons, cubed

3 carrots, halved lengthwise

12–16 baby onions, peeled

6 plum tomatoes, peeled, then thickly sliced

zest of 1 orange, removed in one piece

1 bunch of fresh herbs, such as parsley, thyme, bay leaf, and rosemary, tied with kitchen string

½ cup walnut halves

1 cup robust red wine

2 tablespoons Cognac or brandy

¾ cup beef stock or water

sea salt and freshly ground black pepper

chopped flatleaf parsley, to serve

serves 4–6

To many connoisseurs, brisket is the cut that gives the true, full flavor of beef. No nonsense about having it rare or medium or whatever—this is always well done (and slowly). The meat may be cooked for even longer at a low temperature without any loss of flavor or texture, and some people say the longer, the better. Keep basting and stirring.

brisket & vegetables

3 lb. beef brisket, boned but not rolled

4 onions, cut into chunks

4 carrots, cut into chunks

4 celery ribs, cut into 2-inch slices

your choice of other vegetables, such as parsnips, leeks, and celery root

4 medium potatoes, parboiled and quartered

sea salt and freshly ground black pepper

serves 4–6

Season the meat with salt and pepper and put in a large roasting pan.

Put the pan in a cold oven and turn the temperature to 500°F for the first 40 minutes. This will start the fat running. Add the onions, carrots, celery, and your choice of other vegetables—but not the potatoes. Stir them around to coat with the fat and season lightly with salt and pepper. Reduce the oven temperature to 325°F.

After another 40 minutes, pour in 2 cups hot water, baste the meat, and stir the vegetables with a wooden spoon. Repeat after a further 40 minutes, judging the quantity of water to be added. There should be enough for basting, but the meat should not be awash with liquid. Add the potatoes.

Baste again after another 40 minutes, this time without adding water, and then increase the temperature to 425°F for the last 20 minutes.

Remove the roasting pan from the oven and transfer the meat to a large plate. Keep it warm. Pour off all the liquid from the roasting pan into a fine-mesh sieve and then into a pitcher, leaving most of the fat behind.

Dish up the meat onto a large serving platter with the vegetables around it. Serve the pitcher of gravy separately.

Inspired by thrift, this dish has transcended its humble origins and become a firm favorite around the world. The golden potato topping hides tender lamb in heavenly gravy

lancashire hotpot

Preheat the oven to 350°F.

Heat the oil in a large, flameproof casserole dish, add the lamb, and brown all over. Transfer to a plate. Reduce the heat under the casserole dish, add all the vegetables, then sauté for 10 minutes, stirring frequently.

Remove the casserole from the heat, add the meat, then sprinkle in the flour and mix well. Pour in just enough hot water to cover the meat and vegetables, stir well, and return to the heat.

Bring the casserole to a boil, stirring frequently as the gravy thickens. Season and add the Worcestershire sauce. Remove from the heat.

Slice the potatoes thinly by hand or with a mandolin. Layer them carefully over the meat and vegetables, covering them completely. Place in the oven and cook for 2 hours. The potatoes should be golden on top and the gravy bubbling up around the sides.

2 tablespoons olive oil

2 lb. lamb stewing meat, cut into 2-inch pieces

1 onion, finely diced

2 carrots, finely diced

4 celery ribs, finely diced

2 leeks, thinly sliced

2 tablespoons all-purpose flour

1 tablespoon Worcestershire sauce

2 lb. potatoes, unpeeled

sea salt and freshly ground black pepper

serves 4–6

Think of chilly, dark evenings and this dish is exactly what you would want to eat. The feather-light cheesy dumplings nestling in the rich, savory casserole will have everyone demanding more.

beef & carrot casserole

1 tablespoon olive oil

2 garlic cloves, crushed

1 onion, diced

2 celery ribs, diced

2 lb. chuck steak, cut into cubes

1⅔ cups beef stock

¾ cup red wine

2 bay leaves

2 tablespoons all-purpose flour

4 carrots, cut into small chunks

sea salt and freshly ground black pepper

dumplings

1½ cups all-purpose flour

1 teaspoon baking powder

⅓ cup shortening

½ cup grated sharp Cheddar cheese

serves 4–6

Heat the oil in a large casserole dish, add the garlic, onion, and celery and sauté for 4 minutes. Transfer to a plate. Put the beef in the casserole dish, increase the heat, and sauté for 5 minutes, stirring frequently. When the beef is cooked, return the onion mixture to the casserole dish. Add the stock, red wine, bay leaves, and seasoning, bring to a boil, then reduce the heat to a gentle simmer. Cover and cook for 1½ hours.

To make the dumplings, place the flour and baking powder in a bowl and rub in the shortening until it resembles bread crumbs. Add the cheese, mixing it in with a knife. Add ¼–⅓ cup cold water and use your hands to bring the mixture together and form a dough. Divide into 8 equal pieces and roll into balls.

Remove the casserole dish from the heat for 5 minutes, then sift in the flour and stir to thicken the gravy. Return to the heat, add the carrots, and stir until the casserole comes to a simmer. Place the dumplings on top, cover, and cook for 20 minutes.

Simple dishes are often the best, and they don't come much simpler than this. Long, slow cooking is the secret of the bolognese sauce, which forms the base of the recipe. You can add more or less cayenne pepper, depending on how spicy you like your food. Serve with either bread or boiled rice, and a bowl of guacamole.

chili con carne

Heat the oil in a large saucepan, add the garlic, onions, celery, and carrot and sauté gently for 10 minutes. Add the beef, breaking it up with a wooden spoon, and cook for a further 10 minutes. Add the oregano, thyme, bay leaves, tomato paste, tomato purée, cayenne, paprika, wine, and beans. Season and mix well. Simmer for 1 hour, stirring frequently.

Just before serving, stir in the cilantro. Serve with bread or boiled rice and guacamole.

2 tablespoons olive oil

3 garlic cloves, crushed

2 onions, diced

1 celery rib, diced

1 carrot, diced

1¾ lb. ground beef

a bunch of fresh oregano, chopped

a sprig of thyme

2 bay leaves

2 tablespoons tomato paste

4 cups tomato purée

1 tablespoon cayenne pepper

1 tablespoon paprika

1 glass of red wine

2 x 14-oz. cans red kidney beans, drained and rinsed

a handful of cilantro, chopped

serves 4–6

The inclusion of fish sauce and spices in this beef casserole gives it an unusual Vietnamese flavor. A crusty baguette is an ideal accompaniment for mopping up the juices.

Vietnamese-style beef

1 stalk of lemon grass, peeled and finely chopped

leaves from 3 sprigs of mint, chopped

2 tablespoons fish sauce

1 teaspoon brown sugar

1 inch fresh ginger, peeled and grated

1 red chile, seeded and chopped

2 garlic cloves, crushed

2 lb. boneless beef (foreshank or chuck), cut into 1-inch cubes

2 tablespoons peanut oil

2 tablespoons tomato paste

3 tomatoes, peeled, seeded, and chopped, about 1 lb.

freshly ground black pepper

6 scallions, shredded, to serve

sprigs of mint, to serve

serves 4–6

Put the lemon grass, mint, fish sauce, sugar, ginger, chile, garlic, and lots of freshly ground black pepper in a bowl and mix well.

Add the beef and turn to coat. Cover and marinate in the refrigerator for about 2 hours or overnight.

Heat the oil in a casserole dish, then add the beef in batches and sauté until browned on all sides. Using a slotted spoon, remove each batch to a plate and keep it warm while you cook the remainder.

Return all the beef to the casserole dish, add the tomato paste and tomatoes, and cook for 3–4 minutes until they start to break down. Add 4 cups water and bring to a boil. Reduce the heat and simmer for about 2 hours until the meat is spoon-tender and the sauce rich but not too thick.

Serve in small bowls, topped with shredded scallions and mint sprigs, accompanied by a crusty baguette.

Taking its name from Brunswick County in Virginia, this is a dish designed for a large number of hungry people: it's not sophisticated, just full of goodness. Traditionally, the stew was thickened with mashed potatoes but, in this modern version, they are served separately. Apparently, squirrel used to be one of the ingredients!

brunswick stew

Put the chicken, ham bone or hock, beef, and bay leaf into a large Dutch oven or casserole dish and cover with the stock or water. Do not season unless the hock is unsalted. Cover with a lid, bring to a boil, then reduce the heat, and simmer for about 40 minutes.

Lift out the chicken pieces and ham bone or hock and transfer to a large plate. Let cool and then cut off their meat in chunks and set aside. Discard the bones.

Continue simmering until the beef comes away from the center bone, about 2–4 hours. Discard the bone and add the beef to the chicken and hock.

If necessary, reduce the pan juices to about 3½ cups by boiling hard, then add the onion, tomatoes, celery, lima or fava beans, basil, and parsley. Cover and simmer for about 20 minutes until done.

Return the meats to the casserole dish. If using corn, strip the kernels from the cob and add them to the casserole dish. Add the chile and some pepper, simmer for 5 minutes, taste, and adjust the seasoning. Serve with lots of buttery mashed potatoes.

2 lb. chicken, cut into 4, or 4 leg portions

1 ham bone or uncooked smoked pork hock

1½ lb. shank crosscuts of beef or osso buco

1 bay leaf

7 cups ham stock or water

1 onion, sliced

1 lb. tomatoes, halved, seeded, and chopped

1 celery heart, about 8 oz., chopped

8 oz. green baby lima or fava beans

1½ tablespoons fresh basil, chopped

1½ tablespoons chopped flatleaf parsley

1 ear of fresh corn (optional)

1 red serrano chile, seeded and sliced

sea salt and freshly ground black pepper

serves 8–10

A picnic shoulder of pork is ideal for roasting or braising, as it has just the right amount of fat. A certain amount of fat is needed in this dish to moisten the beans—and the beans are needed to mop up the juices. Either way, it makes for a scrumptious dinner.

pork & bean casserole

¼ cup olive oil

12 oz. carrots, cut into 1-inch chunks

4 onions, peeled but left whole

4 small turnips

1 sprig of thyme

1 bay leaf

6 peppercorns

6 garlic cloves, chopped

4 lb. fresh picnic shoulder of pork

8 oz. thick-cut bacon, cut into chunks

1½ cups canned cannellini beans, drained and rinsed

1½ lb. small potatoes, peeled

8 oz. fresh green beans

sea salt and freshly ground black pepper

serves 4

Preheat the oven to 325°F.

Heat the oil in a large ovenproof casserole dish with a lid, then stir in the carrots, onions, turnips, thyme, bay leaf, peppercorns, and garlic. Gently sauté until softened but not browned.

Meanwhile, cut the rind off the pork and reserve it. Add the pork, its rind, the bacon chunks, and cannellini beans to the casserole dish. Cover with water, add salt and pepper, and bring to a boil on top of the stove. Transfer to the preheated oven and simmer for 1½ hours, or until the beans are tender.

After 1 hour, taste and adjust the seasoning, then add the potatoes for the last 30 minutes and the fresh green beans for the last 5 minutes.

To serve, remove and discard the pork rind, lift the meat onto a dish, and carve into thick slices. Add the vegetables and beans to the dish and serve with a separate small pitcher of the cooking juices.

There are few ingredients in this dish, so the tomatoes must be of premium quality and vine-ripened in the summer sun. Serve with crusty bread for dipping into the rich sauce.

mediterranean lentil stew

Put the lentils in a large saucepan, add sufficient cold water to cover, and set over high heat. Bring to a boil, then reduce the heat and let simmer for 20 minutes until the lentils are tender but retain a little bite. Drain and set aside until needed.

Put the oil in a saucepan set over high heat. Add the onion, garlic, oregano, and pepper flakes and cook for 5 minutes, stirring often, until the onion softens. Add the capers, tomatoes, tomato purée, lentils, and 1 cup water. Bring to a boil, then reduce the heat and let simmer gently for 10 minutes, stirring occasionally.

Spoon into warmed serving dishes, top with the olives and crumbled feta, and serve with crusty bread on the side for dipping into the sauce.

½ cup green or brown lentils

3 tablespoons olive oil

1 onion, chopped

2 garlic cloves, chopped

a small handful of fresh oregano, chopped

1 teaspoon dried hot pepper flakes

1½ tablespoons salted caperberries, rinsed

2 ripe tomatoes, roughly chopped

1 cup tomato purée

2 oz. small black olives, to serve

4 oz. feta cheese, crumbled, to serve

serves 4

In Jamaica, callaloo leaves and yam would be used to make this spicy vegetable stew instead of spinach and sweet potato. A plantain is a large cooking banana (some have delightful pale pink flesh), but you can use ordinary green bananas instead.

caribbean vegetable stew

¼ cup canola or safflower oil

1 white onion, chopped

2 teaspoon ground allspice

1 teaspoon ground cumin

¼ teaspoon freshly grated nutmeg

4 fresh red chiles, seeded and chopped

4 garlic cloves, crushed

2 inches fresh ginger, peeled and grated

5 tomatoes, peeled, seeded, and diced

1 tablespoon chopped flatleaf parsley

2 tablespoons soy sauce

1 sweet potato, peeled and cubed

2 red onions, quartered

2 plantains or green bananas, peeled and cut into chunks

6 baby carrots, trimmed

4 cups baby spinach

1 cup snow peas

freshly ground black pepper

freshly snipped chives, to serve

serves 4

Put the oil in a large, flameproof casserole dish, add the white onion, and cook until softened and translucent. Add the allspice, cumin, nutmeg, chiles, garlic, ginger, tomatoes, and parsley and cook until you reach the consistency of a sauce. Season with the soy sauce.

Add the sweet potato, red onions, and plantains or bananas, cover and simmer for 20 minutes, then add the carrots and spinach and cook for a further 5 minutes, adding the snow peas for the last 2 minutes. Season, scatter with chives, then serve.

one-pot desserts

Plums have such a rich flavor when they are cooked that they need little or no other flavorings with them, except perhaps a pinch of cinnamon. This is a great favorite with kids, especially when made with greeny-red Victoria plums. Try it with greengages, Santa Rosas, or Queen Anne plums—they will all be delicious. For a grown-up crumble, toss the uncooked plums in a little damson or sloe gin.

simple plum crumble

Preheat the oven to 350°F and set a baking sheet on the middle shelf to heat.

Cut the plums in half and remove the pits. Cut the halves into quarters if they are very large. Toss them with the sugar and tip them into an ovenproof baking dish.

To make the crumble topping, rub the butter into the flour with the salt until it resembles rough bread crumbs. Alternatively, do this in a food processor. Stir in the sugar. (At this point the mixture can be placed into a plastic bag and chilled until ready to cook.)

Lightly scatter the topping mixture over the plums. Place the baking dish on the baking sheet in the preheated oven and bake for 40–45 minutes, until golden brown.

Remove from the oven and serve warm with light cream.

8–10 ripe plums

4–5 tablespoons sugar

crumble topping

½ stick plus 1 tablespoon unsalted butter, chilled

1⅓ cups all-purpose flour

a pinch of salt

¼ cup superfine sugar

light cream, to serve

serves 4–6

The word "slump" seems to describe perfectly the sloppy batter that covers the seasonal fruit in this satisfying dessert. Any juicy fruit or berries can be used, and you can substitute pine nuts for almonds and sprinkle them all over the batter. You can also add a drop or two of almond extract to the batter if you like a stronger flavor.

apricot & almond slump

1 lb. 6 oz. fresh apricots

½ cup light brown sugar

almond slump batter

1½ cups all-purpose flour

1 tablespoon baking powder

a pinch of salt

¼ cup light brown sugar

1 cup ground almonds

about 1½ cups milk (not fat-free)

½ stick unsalted butter, melted

¼ cup whole blanched almonds

vanilla ice cream, to serve

serves 4–6

Preheat the oven to 375°F.

Cut the apricots in half, remove the pits, and mix with the sugar. Set aside until needed.

To make the batter, sift together the flour, baking powder, and salt, and mix with the sugar in a bowl. Stir in the ground almonds, milk, and melted butter and whisk until smooth and thick. Pour the batter into a large, lightly buttered baking pan, then push in the apricots cut side up, but in a higgledy-piggledy manner and slightly at an angle all over. Place a whole almond inside each apricot where the pit once was.

Bake the slump for 25–30 minutes in the middle of the preheated oven, until risen and golden.

Remove from the oven and allow to cool slightly before serving with vanilla ice cream.

Ripe figs need almost nothing done to them—but if you bake them with lots of vanilla and lemon-scented sugar, and hide a walnut in the middle of each one, you will end up with something divine! Take care not to overcook them or they will collapse.

figs baked with vanilla & lemon

Preheat the oven to 450°F.

Cut a deep cross in the top of each fig so that they open up a little. Push a walnut half into each cross. Pack the figs closely together in a shallow baking dish.

Chop the vanilla beans and put into a food processor. Add the sugar and lemon zest and process until the beans and zest are chopped into tiny bits. Spoon the mixture over each fig and around the dish. Moisten with white wine.

Bake in the preheated oven for 10 minutes until the sugar melts and the figs start to caramelize. Remove from the oven and let cool for a few minutes before serving with cream. Alternatively, serve cold with ice cream.

12 large ripe figs

12 walnut halves

2 plump vanilla beans

⅔ cup sugar

grated zest from 1 unwaxed lemon

3 tablespoons white wine

heavy ceam or ice cream, to serve

serves 6

This is one of the best ways of cooking pears—it is so simple to make, yet tastes very luxurious. Choose pears that are ripe but not too soft, or they will overcook in the oven. If you can't get a good rich Marsala or Vin Santo, use sweet sherry or Madeira instead.

caramelized pears

6 large ripe pears

¾ cup superfine sugar

⅔ cup Marsala or Vin Santo

8 oz. mascarpone cheese

1 vanilla bean, split, seeds scraped out and reserved

serves 6

Preheat the oven to 375°F.

Cut the pears in half and scoop out the cores—do not peel them. Sprinkle the sugar into a flameproof, ovenproof pan or dish. Set over medium heat and let the sugar melt and caramelize. Remove from the heat as soon as it reaches a medium-brown color and quickly arrange the pears cut side down in the caramel.

Bake in the preheated oven until the pears are soft, 20–25 minutes. Carefully lift out the pears and set aside, keeping the caramel in the pan.

Put the pan on top of the stove over medium heat and add the Marsala or Vin Santo. Bring to a boil, stirring to dislodge any set caramel, and boil fast until reduced and syrupy. Set aside.

Scoop out a good teaspoon from each cooked pear and put it in a bowl. Add the mascarpone and vanilla seeds and beat well. Fill the centers of the pears with the mascarpone mixture. Return to the oven for 5 minutes until the mascarpone has heated through. Serve with the caramel sauce spooned over the top.

Using frozen summer berries for this recipe is convenient and also means that you can make it year-round. Serve with crunchy biscuits such as biscotti.

spiced berry compote

Put the frozen berries in a saucepan with the sugar, cinnamon, and 2 tablespoons of water. Cover and simmer for 5 minutes or until the berries have defrosted and are juicy.

Blend the cornstarch or arrowroot with a little cold water, then mix into the pan. Heat, stirring, until the compote has thickened. Pour into a bowl and let cool.

Serve the compote lightly swirled into the yogurt, with biscotti on the side, if you wish.

2⅔ cups frozen mixed berries

2 tablespoons superfine sugar

a pinch of ground cinnamon or 1 cinnamon stick

2 teaspoons cornstarch or arrowroot

2½ cups Greek (strained) yogurt, to serve

serves 4

This is a pretty marbled dessert of crushed raspberries with a luxurious hint of white chocolate. To make the recipe lighter, you can use low-fat yogurt.

white chocolate & raspberry fool

1½ oz. white chocolate

1 cup fresh raspberries

¾ cup Greek (strained) yogurt

serves 2

Chop the chocolate and put in a heatproof bowl set over a saucepan of gently simmering water until melted. Remove from the heat and let cool for a couple of minutes.

Reserve 6 raspberries to decorate, then roughly crush the remaining raspberries with a fork.

Mix the yogurt into the melted chocolate, then gently fold in the crushed raspberries to give a marbled effect. Spoon into 2 glasses and decorate with the reserved raspberries. Cover and chill in the refrigerator until ready to serve.

These soft, pear-shaped fruits have a sweet, honey-nectar flavor that is lovely with cured meats and cheese. Once picked, they ripen very quickly, and late-season figs are perfect cooked in puddings.

fig & honey croissant pudding

Preheat the oven to 350°F.

Put the croissant pieces in the bottom of a lightly greased baking dish. Arrange the fig halves in between the croissant pieces and drizzle the honey over the top.

Combine the eggs, milk, light cream, and sugar in a bowl and pour into the dish. Let stand for about 20 minutes so that the croissants can absorb some of the custard. Bake in the preheated oven for 50 minutes, until the top of the pudding is a dark golden brown.

Let cool a little before cutting into slices and serving with dollops of heavy ceam on the side.

Variation When figs aren't in season, you can lightly spread each piece of croissant with some good-quality fig jelly before putting into the dish. Leave out the honey and add ⅓ cup slivered almonds to the egg mixture instead.

2 croissants, preferably stale, each torn into 6 pieces

6 fresh figs, halved

¼ cup clear honey

3 eggs

1 cup whole milk

1 cup light cream

¼ cup superfine sugar

heavy ceam, to serve

serves 4

Baked fruit may seem old-fashioned and stodgy, but not these, especially if you use a crisp eating apple. This recipe is sheer heaven and perhaps the easiest cooked dessert you will ever make. Allow one small apple and half a pear per person.

baked apples & pears

2 apples, preferably Rome Beauty or Braeburn

1 just-ripe pear

4 tablespoons whole hazelnuts, coarsely chopped

6 soft prunes, chopped

4–5 dried figs, chopped

a pinch of ground cinnamon

4 tablespoons unsalted butter

4 teaspoons clear honey

plain thick yogurt, to serve

serves 2

Preheat the oven to 400°F.

Peel the apples. If necessary, trim the bottom slightly so they sit flat. Remove the cores with a small knife or a corer. Using a small spoon, scrape out some apple to make space for more stuffing. Don't go all the way down to the bottom. Peel the pear, then cut in half and scoop out the core, as for the apple.

Put the hazelnuts, prunes, and figs in a small bowl and stir well.

Arrange the apples and pears in a baking dish. Stuff the nut mixture into the apple and pear cavities, mounding it at the top. Top each with a light sprinkling of cinnamon, 1 tablespoon butter, and trickle over a teaspoon or so of honey. Cover with foil.

Bake in the preheated oven for 20 minutes, then remove the foil and continue baking until just golden, 10–15 minutes more. Divide the apples and pears carefully between the plates and pour over any pan juices. Serve warm, with plain yogurt.

This is an American classic but made here with sour cream instead of traditional buttermilk. It should be eaten soon after baking because the dough soaks up the fruit juices. Add a basket of blackberries to the peaches, if you like, or use a combination of peaches, apricots, and blackberries.

peach cobbler

Preheat the oven to 375°F.

Cut the peaches in half, remove the pits, then cut each half into 3 slices. Put them in a shallow baking dish, sprinkle with the flour, and toss well to coat evenly. Add the lemon juice and honey and stir. Set aside.

To make the topping, put the cream and sour cream in a large bowl and stir well. Set aside.

Put the flour, sugar, baking powder, baking soda, and salt in a large bowl and mix well. Add the butter and mix with your fingertips until the mixture resembles coarse crumbs. Using a fork, stir in the cream mixture until blended—use your hands at the end if necessary—the mixture should be sticky, thick, and not willing to blend easily.

Drop spoonfuls of the mixture on top of the peaches, leaving gaps to expose the fruit. Sprinkle sugar liberally on top of the batter. Bake in the preheated oven until golden, 25–35 minutes. Serve warm with cream or ice cream.

6 peaches, not too ripe

1 tablespoon all-purpose flour

1 tablespoon freshly squeezed lemon juice

3 tablespoons clear honey

cream or vanilla ice cream, to serve

cobbler topping

½ cup heavy ceam

⅓ cup sour cream

1¼ cups all-purpose flour

¼ cup sugar, plus extra for sprinkling

1 teaspoon baking powder

¼ teaspoon baking soda

a pinch of salt

4 tablespoons unsalted butter

2–3 tablespoons sugar, for sprinkling

serves 6

index

conversion charts

Weights and measures have been rounded up or down slightly to make measuring easier.

Volume equivalents:

American	Metric	Imperial
1 teaspoon	5 ml	
1 tablespoon	15 ml	
¼ cup	60 ml	2 fl.oz.
⅓ cup	75 ml	2½ fl.oz.
½ cup	125 ml	4 fl.oz.
⅔ cup	150 ml	5 fl.oz. (¼ pint)
¾ cup	175 ml	6 fl.oz.
1 cup	250 ml	8 fl.oz.
1 stick butter = 8 tablespoons = 125 g		

Weight equivalents:

Imperial	Metric
1 oz.	25 g
2 oz.	50 g
3 oz.	75 g
4 oz.	125 g
5 oz.	150 g
6 oz.	175 g
7 oz.	200 g
8 oz. (½ lb.)	250 g
9 oz.	275 g
10 oz.	300 g
11 oz.	325 g
12 oz.	375 g
13 oz.	400 g
14 oz.	425 g
15 oz.	475 g
16 oz. (1 lb.)	500 g
2 lb.	1 kg

Measurements:

Inches	Cm
¼ inch	5 mm
½ inch	1 cm
¾ inch	1.5 cm
1 inch	2.5 cm
2 inches	5 cm
3 inches	7 cm
4 inches	10 cm
5 inches	12 cm
6 inches	15 cm
7 inches	18 cm
8 inches	20 cm
9 inches	23 cm
10 inches	25 cm
11 inches	28 cm
12 inches	30 cm

Oven temperatures:

110°C	(225°F)	Gas ¼
120°C	(250°F)	Gas ½
140°C	(275°F)	Gas 1
150°C	(300°F)	Gas 2
160°C	(325°F)	Gas 3
180°C	(350°F)	Gas 4
190°C	(375°F)	Gas 5
200°C	(400°F)	Gas 6
220°C	(425°F)	Gas 7
230°C	(450°F)	Gas 8
240°C	(475°F)	Gas 9

recipe credits

Nadia Arumguram
Chicken & yellow
  bean stir-fry
Chinese lemon
  chicken
Five-spice duck
Jasmine rice with
  crab & asparagus
Spiced mixed
  vegetables
Thai-flavor pork
Tofu & mushroom
  noodles

Ghillie Basan
Chicken & olive tagine
Spicy chicken tagine
Summer tagine of
  lamb
Tagine of baby
  eggplant

Fiona Beckett
Chicken with white
  wine

Maxine Clark
Apricot & almond
  slump
Artichoke & pecorino
  risotto
Bacon & eggs in a pan
Caramelized pears
Figs baked with vanilla
  & lemon
Green herb risotto
Potato & mushroom
  gratin
Ratatouille
Saffron potato salad
Simple plum crumble
Squash blossom
  risotto
Wild mushroom
  risotto

Ross Dobson
Creamy vegetable
  curry
Eggplant, tomato,
  & lentil curry

Fig & honey croissant
  pudding
Lemony chicken with
  leeks
Mediterranean lentil
  stew
Orange vegetable pilaf
Roasted vegetables
  & chickpeas
Smoky hotpot
Tabbouleh with
  chickpeas
Vegetarian paella

Clare Ferguson
Boeuf en daube
Camargue chicken
Chicken & pork paella
Spanish potato omelet

Silvana Franco
Oven-roasted spicy
  macaroni

Liz Franklin
Bang-bang chicken
Italian vegetable
  & bread soup
Marinated mushrooms
Poulet sauté au
  vinaigre

Tonia George
Chicken & lentil curry
Harrira
Lamb & fava bean
  tagine
Lentil, spinach, &
  cumin soup
Minestrone
Pad thai
Red curry with shrimp
  & pumpkin
Stir-fried asparagus
  & tofu
Sweet potato salad
Tomato soup

Rachael Anne Hill
Chicken & barley
  supper
Mackerel & bulgur
  wheat salad
Moroccan honey
  & lemon chicken
Mustardy mushroom
  stroganoff
Saffron fish pilaf
Shrimp & lima bean
  rice
Spiced berry compote
White chocolate
  & raspberry fool

**Elsa Petersen-
Schepelern**
Baked stuffed
  pumpkin
Italian tuna & beans
Spicy butternut
  & chicken curry

Louise Pickford
Gingered chicken
  noodles
Pasta with melted
  ricotta
Thai-style beef salad

Jennie Shapter
Artichoke & ham
  tortilla
Chickpea tortilla
Feta cheese & tomato
  open omelet
Paella tortilla
Porcini frittata
Sun-dried tomato
  frittata

Sonia Stevenson
Braised lamb with okra
Brisket & vegetables
Brunswick stew
Caribbean vegetable
  stew
Fish mollee
Pork & bean casserole

Roast cod cutlets
Spicy chickpeas
Vietnamese-style beef

Linda Tubby
Baked rice with garlic
Baked sardines
Imam bayildi
Tuna & potato stew

Sunil Vijayakar
Beef madras
Red kidney bean curry

Fran Warde
Beef & carrot
  casserole
Bouillabaisse
Chicken & bacon pot
Chili con carne
Easy fish stew
Lamb navarin
Lamb pilaf
Lancashire hotpot
Tuna patties

Laura Washburn
Baked apples & pears
Bell pepper & chorizo
  tortilla
Chicken, sausage,
  & rice
Creamy potato gratin
Greek-style omelet
Lamb stew with piri
  piri
Peach cobbler
Shrimp with couscous
Spring lamb stew

photography credits

Key: a=above, b=below, r=right, l=left, c=center.

Caroline Arber
Pages 26, 117, 183,
200, 203, 204

Henry Bourne
Pages 15, 210

Martin Brigdale
Pages 6ac, 55, 62, 88r,
90, 93, 94, 95, 97, 103,
105, 110, 112, 118l,
118r, 120, 121, 123,
124, 128, 129, 142,
150, 151, 152, 156,
166c, 167, 168, 176,
191, 193

Peter Cassidy
Pages 6c, 6cr, 7, 16,
29, 36, 38, 43, 50, 57,
66, 85, 107, 108, 137,
146r, 147, 154, 155,
162, 164, 165, 170,
196, 218, 219, 220,
221, 222, 223, 225,
227

Nicki Dowey
Pages 88l, 113, 166r,
187

Tara Fisher
Pages 6ar, 46 all, 56,
59, 60, 63, 64, 67, 115

Caroline Hughes
Page 125

Richard Jung
Pages 2-3, 6al, 6cl, 6bl,
6bc, 8l, 8c, 9, 14, 25,
41, 68 all, 69, 70, 71,
73, 74, 77, 78, 81, 83,
88c, 89, 98, 102, 106,
109, 119, 139, 140,
146c, 159, 160, 166l,
174, 175, 180, 186,
212, 216r, 217, 230,
231

William Lingwood
Pages 4-5, 45, 143,
146l, 148, 179, 181,
195, 199, 207, 208,
211, 215

Diana Miller
Pages 27, 37, 76

David Munns
Pages 6br, 47, 51, 52,
101, 172, 188, 216l,
233, 234

Noel Murphy
Pages 22, 48, 114

William Reveall
Pages 8r, 30, 32, 33,
42, 82, 86, 87, 127,
131, 132, 133, 158,
184, 216c, 226, 229

Craig Robertson
Page 197

Yuki Sugiura
Pages 1, 10, 13, 17,
18

Debi Treloar
Pages 21, 144, 163,
171, 192

Pia Tryde
Pages 28, 92

Ian Wallace
Page 34

Kate Whitaker
Pages 118c, 135, 136

Francesca Yorke
Page 235